# Unwrapping Your Gift

## Thirty Steps to Becoming the Successful Person You Are Meant to Be!

By Giulio Veglio

Illustrated By Glenn Brown

**Unwrapping Your Gift**

Copyright © 2013 by Giulio Veglio

ISBN 9780986515767

Published by Visionary Freak Media,
and imprint of Visionary Freak LLC
29 Jay Street #1075
Schenectady, NY 12301
866-998-4226

Illustrated by Glenn Brown
Edited by Rick Mickelson, AwareNow Publishing, www.awarenow.ca, Typesetting by L.B. Word Works, and Published by Visionary Freak Media.

Visit us on the web!
www.visionaryfreak.com

"'BRILLANT!' Incorporating Giulio Veglio's 30 simple steps into your daily life will help you achieve inspiring results."

**Winn Claybaugh**
Author of BE NICE (OR ELSE!)
Dean & Cofounder of Paul Mitchell Schools

Unwrapping Your Gift

# CONTENTS

# Unwrapping Your Gift

# FOREWORD

I have had the privilege and honor of knowing Giulio Veglio for many years as he has been in our Education Program as a Master Educator and Speaker since 1985. From the beginning, Giulio has always been a top platform artist and teacher for John Paul Mitchell Systems.

In January of 2000, we had the wonderful opportunity of partnering with Giulio in a Paul Mitchell School. Over the years we have joined forces with him in many other schools. Through our many successful associations, I really got to know, understand and enjoy Giulio and we became true friends

We share a very common bond. As you probably know from reading Giulio's first book, *A Slap On The Back Of The Head*, he came to this country from Italy as a young boy and was raised in the United States. I was born in the U.S. but my parents were Italian so both Guilio and I grew up exposed to strong Italian values. We also have much in common on a personal level and often find ourselves saying "it's the Italian thing", when we share the same thoughts and reactions. We have both been very blessed with these cultural values and they reflect what happens in our everyday interactions.

I have been able to spend quality time with Giulio and really got to know him at a profound level, as both a friend and business partner. He is fun, motivating, driven, loving and passionate. These qualities make him a successful businessman and parent. He is the kind of positive person everyone loves to be around. He's always smiling and making you feel like you're one of his best friends. His world revolves around family and when I say "family" I'm not just referring to his blood relatives. Almost everyone he meets eventually becomes his "family". If you are fortunate enough to spend time with him you'll understand exactly what I mean.

Until this happens, his love, passion, sharing and caring will come out to you in his words, should you be so lucky as to read his books.

*Unwrapping Your Gifts* is a book that conveys some powerful stories as well as a call to action regarding the special gifts we have all been given by our Creator. These gifts also reflect what made Giulio so successful and turned him into the amazing man he is today. Describing the gifts also offers us all many important lessons to meditate on within our own lives.

I am certain you will find this book as delightful and distinctive as the author, a person I am proud to call a colleague and a friend.

Luke Jacobellis
President, John Paul Mitchell Systems

# INTRODUCTION

I have a confession to make up front. I am obsessed with uncovering the "tricks" to success. I have studied successful people my whole life, mostly because I really didn't think I'd be one of them. Then, after I started reaching so many of my goals, people wanted to know how I did it.

As an Italian immigrant, I was pushed through the American school system starting at the age of five. I barely graduated from high school but ultimately I became a successful business owner, a popular motivational speaker and an award-winning author.

Some people think that they'll never be successful because they just don't have good luck. Then there's the school of thought that you have to be in the right place at the right time or you just won't ever see success. Another common belief is that unless your family has a lot of money, you won't.

**The reality is that YOU create your success. YOU have the power to achieve the goals you set for yourself. YOU control your destiny. YOU can do whatever you dream you can do.**

As I travel all over the country giving seminars, I'm often asked,

"Giulio, why is it that I can't achieve the goals I want to achieve? What is it that's stopping me from getting where I want to go?" Or my favorite, "Why can't I just win the lottery?"

While I'll agree that some people seem to have "all the luck," I want you to know that you can "create" all the "luck" you want, too. Success isn't as tricky as I'd once thought. It's really just a matter of changing attitudes, mindsets and habits. This sounds like an uphill climb that will take years, but it can be accomplished in just a few short weeks.

The more successful people I study, the more I see that they all use the same patterns to achieve their goals. I've broken down my years of observation into thirty steps that I have personally followed to create my own success and I am excited to share them with you. I wrote this book to give you a simple, effective process that is guaranteed to create a new you.

I know what you're thinking:

"Thirty steps will take forever!"

Don't let the number of steps overwhelm you before you even get started. I promise you that you will move through the steps quickly. I'm going to break them down slowly, but as you use them, you're going to notice that one leads to another. They all work together because you've actually done it all before. You just weren't aware of it. I want to make you conscious about it so you know exactly what you did and you can repeat it over and over again. Since you're going to have many goals in your life, this process will come in handy.

Many people sit around waiting for life to happen but you are not one of those people. I know this by the fact that you have this book. You wouldn't have read this far if you didn't have dreams somewhere inside of you just waiting to be released.

It's time to get moving towards living your wildest dreams and realizing your full potential. This is your moment to "unwrap your gifts"!

# GETTING READY TO UNWRAP YOUR GIFTS

Think of this as your "workbook to success." This is NOT one of those books featuring a bunch of great ideas that you read and then put down never to implement. This is an action-oriented, proactive process so let's talk about how to approach the steps to unwrapping your gifts.

I recommend that you get some simple supplies. You'll need an empty binder and a pen. There are worksheets that coordinate with each of the thirty steps available for downloading at www.visionaryfreak.com/worksheets, or you can go ahead and write directly in this book. It's okay!

Don't make the mistake of skipping the written exercises at the end of each step. They are brief, but powerful and will keep you accountable and driven to action. In my years of observation, I've noticed that successful people do take the time to make and keep notes about their journeys so that they have a record of what worked and what didn't. These exercises will help you get to the next level of success.

Another thing I'd suggest is to share the ideas in this book with other people. It's a great thing to do with your staff, your friends, your family – and even your kids. This offers the added bonus of helping reinforce what you are learning while potentially making an impact on others' lives.

Let's do one exercise right now, so you can get the idea of what I'm talking about. It's easy and it won't take long (none of the exercises do). Grab your notebook. Write a negative thought about yourself. It should be something that you've been dwelling on or that's prevented you from becoming successful in the past.

Be honest with yourself. You can't change your patterns unless you start becoming honest with who you are and what you think. What is that negative thought?

After you write it down, read through this next paragraph. Then I want you to close your eyes and visualize how it's affected you in the past, how it's affecting you in the present and how ultimately it will affect you in the future. Go ahead. Do you like what you see? How does this make you feel right now?

Are you feeling anxious, depressed and sad? How are you starting to react to this before you even start doing it? So, why are you dwelling on it?

What do you think your negative thoughts do to you? All of a sudden you're feeling great, pumped, motivated and ready to go to that next level and "BAM" – negativity comes into your life.

This is one exercise that you have my permission to get rid of. In fact, rip out that piece of paper that you had your negative thoughts on and crumple it up because you don't need it anymore. I want you to learn from it and move on.

### Now, let's get more positive!!!

Get your worksheet – either the one you downloaded or the one right in this book and write down at least one positive thought about yourself. I did say "at least," so if you can come up with more than one, go for it. Ultimately, it would be great for you to fill an entire page, but for now, let's focus on at least one.

The only rules are that it has to be true and you have to believe it.

Here are some examples:

- ☒ I have cute toes.
- ☒ I'm a wonderful mom.
- ☒ I'm a great lover.
- ☒ I'm a fabulous friend.
- ☒ I've got a great butt.

After you write them down, turn on some fun music and close your eyes. Visualize how you *felt* when you thought about the positive thoughts you just wrote down.

When you keep thinking these positive thoughts, how's it going to affect your present as well as your future? When you begin thinking differently about yourself, you will begin acting differently, too. You'll notice that things seem a bit brighter and you get less frustrated with yourself.

As you focus on these positive thoughts, your negative thoughts are going to try to sneak back. DO NOT let them in. You've already thrown them out, so don't dig through the trash and pull out the rotten thoughts!

Get back to those positive thoughts and feel their energy. Feel the love and enjoy it. Every time I do this exercise in my seminars, I am amazed to see what happens. When people write negative thoughts, they won't share them with anyone. It's personal and there may even be some shame associated with those thoughts. The room gets quiet. You can hear a pin drop.

However, when it comes time to write down the positive thoughts, you should see the transformations. While I have fun music playing in the background, the magic begins when everyone starts writing down uplifting thoughts. The level of chatter increases because people start sharing with anyone who will listen. I hear laughter and see people smiling and hugging.

Keep the list of positive thoughts about yourself with you at all times. Add to it as often as possible. I'd love it if you had to use more than one page! Read it every morning, every time you get into a negative state of mind and every time you go to bed. We will use this list several times throughout our "thirty steps to a more successful you"!

Are you starting to feel positive about yourself? You should because you are a very special person. You have gifts that have been given to you by your Creator that you haven't tapped into yet. They will take you to where you want to go. You just need to start unwrapping them NOW. See what happens.

Let's get started!

# Unwrapping Your Gift

## Step 1: Stop Procrastinating

Procrastination causes anxiety, laziness, pain and fear. On any given day, you may have a dozen projects going on in your life. Besides work, these might include paying bills, projects around the house, running errands in your home town or completing school assignments. In addition to all the predictable ones, you may get surprised by last minute things like rounding up a birthday card, picking up a friend with car trouble or dealing with a crashed hard drive on your computer. These experiences can make you feel overwhelmed. How can you get everything done in one day? At some point, you start taking shortcuts and say,

"I'll do it tomorrow."

My father used to say to me,

"With you, tomorrow never comes."

It took me a long time to get anything done. If he asked me to mow the lawn, it would always be done "tomorrow."

I used to be the world's worst procrastinator. If I'm not careful, I still am! When you keep putting things off, what starts as a handful of projects on your list suddenly feels like a thousand tasks. As time goes on, everything seems to be getting more and more overwhelming. In fact, I'm totally stressed-out just writing about it! That's why I want to address the need to prioritize.

## What To Do

You have to prioritize! Start by deciding what is most important; that is to say, what has to get done today. This means if you don't do it today everything will collapse – your business, your studies and your exercises. What is that one task that must come first – a phone call, a letter or a bill? What is the most important thing that needs to get done today? Everything else can wait for another day.

Of course, not everything on your list is going to be critically important. I know each task seems to be more important than the last, but there *are* ways to figure out how to separate them.

Have you ever seen how wine is made? One of the first steps is to put fresh, plump, beautiful grapes into a barrel and squeeze all the delicious juice out of them, leaving the bitter skins in the barrel. My wine-barrel method of prioritizing is similar.

Let's say you have ten things to do tomorrow. In addition to those things, you have to put in an eight hour work day and attend a class that night. Needless to say, it's going to be tough to get those ten things done, right? This is where prioritizing makes your life function so much better.

Turn to the worksheet at the end of this chapter, and download it from the website. Then create a list of the things you have to get done tomorrow. Put everything in the section above the barrel, including your work and classes.

Inside the barrel is where the wine gets processed and that is where your list gets processed, too. We get ourselves all tied up in knots thinking we absolutely HAVE to do it all. Let's sort through it and discover ways to do it better.

Under the barrel, in the left column labeled "Urgent", write the items from the top list that absolutely can't be moved, beginning with the class and your work day. **This is a process I call "funneling".**

Now look at everything in the top column and see if there's anything there that you must complete today, such as paying the electric bill. For me, this would be considered urgent, especially since I don't like it when the electricity is shut off. I'm not happy being in the dark.

Those things get written on the left hand "must do" column, too. Now make sure you're not overloading yourself. Can you really fit it all in? Are there things you can delegate to others?

Anything you can delegate to someone else or delay until next week should be written in the column labeled "Important." You can push those items to another day or ask someone else to do them.

Now look at your list again. What else is on it that has to be done today? Write all of those things in the "Urgent" column. Really look at those things closely. Can any of them get moved to another day of the week, or even another week? Are there any items there that are "nice to-dos", in other words things that don't absolutely HAVE to be done?

Your "Nice to-Dos" need to be left until you have free time. They get written on the right list under the barrel. There may be days where the something on the "Urgent" list suddenly gets replaced with an item that has to take priority.

Set up a regular time to complete your "must do" list. This would be a time when there are not going to be any interruptions. I do this in the morning before my day starts and before the phone rings. But it could be at night when you shut the phone and computer off at a specific time so you can prioritize the tasks for the upcoming day. You must know how much time you need to get all those items done.

Go to the Store
Homework
Pay Bills
Pick Up Kids

URGENT  IMPORTANT  NICE-TO-DOS

_____     _____     _____

_____     _____     _____

_____     _____     _____

_____     _____     _____

Keep that paper with you and add to it as things arise. You'd be surprised how much you can get done once you're on a roll. This happens when you know exactly what needs to happen. Prioritize and stop procrastinating!

If you fail to prepare, then **PREPARE** to fail.

# Unwrapping Your Gift

## Step 2: Finish What You Start

There is a difference between finishing what you start and procrastinating. Finishing what you start shows you've started the project. But even though you get started, you may not follow through to completion. When you keep putting things off procrastination raises its ugly head.

On the other hand, completing a task gives you a feeling of success. When you're finished you have less stress, anxiety and negative emotions. There's a sense of accomplishment in your mind and you now have one less thing to worry about.

Many people get started on a variety of great plans but end up not following through and not reaping any rewards. I used to get caught in that vicious cycle myself – but I sure know better now.

Do any of these situations sound familiar? You rushed out and bought that new treadmill but now observe it in your bedroom with clothes piled all over it. You enrolled in a year's gym membership but have only gone twice. You built the raised bed for your new organic garden but now it sits waiting for the plants. You got a great motivational book from the library that was going to change your life but now it's due back and you only read one chapter. The list goes on. Whatever you started but didn't finish weighs heavily on your mind. For some reason it's easier to make excuses than to be fully accountable. But, we're not fooling anyone – least of all ourselves.

Finish what you start. Stay focused on completing it until it's done. There are going to be things that hinder your progress. However, you still need to go back to what you started and finish them all. Put a time limit on all your tasks and stay on track.

## **What To Do**

In Step 1 we focused on starting. Now let's focus on finishing:

- ☒ Go back to the procrastination exercise you did in Step 1.

- ☒ Write down three things that you finished.

  _____

  _____

  _____

  _____

- ☒ Check them off and share them with people. Make each one a big celebration.

- ☒ Do one thing at a time, check it off then start on the next thing.

- ☒ Revisit your list every month to make sure you are finishing everything you start.

Notes:

_____

_____

_____

_____

_____

I often find that an accountability partner makes all the difference between succeeding and not succeeding in accomplishing your goals. Find someone who has some goals to accomplish and set a time to meet every week or two to hold each other accountable for reaching the goals you've set.

# Unwrapping Your Gift

## Step 3: Take Action

In 1986, I was at a critical time in my life. I had a serious addiction and it was time to clean up my act.

I sat my parents down and together we made some action plans. We decided that I needed to get away from all the negative influences enabling my addiction. I fully accepted that this was necessary. I took action by going to Italy.

It wasn't easy being in another country because I really didn't have any connections or support systems in place. Since I wanted to become an amazing hairstylist, I realized I needed more education. As fate would have it, I met an Italian salon owner who took an interest in my goals. The next thing I knew I was working at his salon. Surprising what happens when you share your dreams.

I worked there during the day. At night I attended school. After a year in Milan getting sober, cleaning myself up and broadening my education, I came back to the U.S. and started over again. I didn't wait for people to ask me about my time abroad. The first thing I did was network and look for opportunities to share my education and experience. I wanted to help other stylists. Since I wanted to become an educator, I was told to check out Paul Mitchell Systems. That suggestion changed my life. I have been connected with the company ever since.

As I worked my way up within Paul Mitchell Systems, I didn't wait for the artistic directors to discover me. I would go to shows and sneak back stage looking for ways to make myself known. When I saw a working artist who interested me, I would just grab a brush and start assisting.

In this way I was able to get invaluable exposure. As a result, I was hired to perform in these shows. Eventually, I started becoming a keynote speaker instead of just the "warm-up" act!

When I came to face to face with my addiction, I never dreamed where I would end up. My journey was unbelievable and put me on the road to great successes. Why? I took action. If you are waiting for success to find you, it won't. You must find it. You have to get out there and take action.

## What To Do

What have you been waiting to do in your life? When I ask you this question, what immediately comes to your mind?

1.  Write down the first thing that comes to mind when I ask you what you've been waiting for.

    _____

    _____

    _____

2.  Write down three things that need to happen for that to take place.

    _____

    _____

    _____

3.  Now, what can you do to take action? Start with one thing and take action. Identify it and take action. It's yours.

    _____

    _____

    _____

If you don't get it the first time, go after it again and again. "No" just means "not now".

Giulio's Gift

Find your passion and take action.

ANYTHING & EVERYTHING IS POSSIBLE!

# Unwrapping Your Gift

## Step 4:  Ask for Help

Ask and you shall receive. How many times have you heard this saying and dismissed it? If you don't take the first step and ask, you will never have the chance to receive.

The good news is that there is somebody out there who's willing to help you do whatever you need done – and even go the extra mile for you. If you need to learn a new software program, ask someone to show you the ropes. If you want to change jobs, ask others to help you network. If you need help to achieve a specific goal, ask someone in the know. What's the worst they can say? No? I've been told "no" thousands of times and look at me. I survived, lived to tell about it and flourished. It's no big deal.

If you know there's something in your life that's not right, I urge you to ask for help. For example, if you are drinking alcohol or using illegal drugs, there are a variety of options available to support you. I know many people who are afraid to admit that they are anxious or depressed. Take it from one who learned the hard way – don't be ashamed, it's okay to ask for help.

We're all afraid to ask for help because we've been conditioned that it's a sign of weakness to do so. That's baloney! I need help constantly as do most people. We can't achieve everything or give up all our bad habits by ourselves. We do need help. In some cases you just have to put your pride aside and say,

"Hey, I really need help."

## What To Do

1. Pick something that you feel is not your strength or something you want to do well. You may be good at it but you want to be excellent at it.

   _____

   _____

   _____

2. Write down the things you can do to improve.

   _____

   _____

   _____

3. Identify three people you know are experts in the areas you want to excel.

   _____

   _____

   _____

I often see friends seeking relationship advice from people who can't maintain their own marriages. Perhaps these experts have been divorced several times. That's not the kind of expert I have in mind! If you want relationship advice, find a couple that have been married for fifty years. **ASK FOR HELP FROM PEOPLE WHO KNOW!**

# Unwrapping Your Gift

# Step 5: Dress up and Stand Tall

People will make judgments about you in the first few seconds that they meet you. Think about how *you* form first impressions of the people you meet.

You may say,

"Wow, she's hot! She seems so mature and professional."

The way people first appear to you forms the basis for your judgments of them. You may decide that they are sharp and impressive with-out really knowing them at all. In reality it is not wise to judge people – but it's what we all do.

If you go to a hairdresser who can't take care of his own hair, how confident are you that he will take care of yours? Would you go to a dentist who has no teeth?

Even the smartest scam-artist knows that appearance is everything. If he wants to trick you the way he dresses, talks and behaves is going to get you to buy into who he is.

I'm not advocating that you dress to fool people but you get my point. I want to focus on the positive side on why it is important for you to dress up and stand tall. It has been proven that those who take care of themselves will take care of their business and take care of their customers.

Let's face it, when we dress up we act differently. Kids even behave differently. Studies show that in secondary schools on picture taking day, there are fewer kids in the principal's office for disciplinary actions than any other day. Maybe we should dress our kids up every day!

When we dress up, we feel empowered. It's like the difference between wearing sweatpants and casual clothes or a designer outfit. Dressing up doesn't mean you have to spend a fortune on clothes. It means that you just make the best of what you have. You don't have to spend a million dollars but you can look like a million dollars by just accessorizing the right clothes.

Whether you go to Wal-Mart, Marshalls or Macy's, you can find great bargains on clothes and accessories. Every store has a sales rack! Some of my best compliments have come when I wear no-brand, less expensive suits. Anything is possible as long as you know how to mix and match. And if you don't, well, there are people out there that are willing to help you.

When you go shopping, here's a trick I like to share. Make sure you pick the sales person that you feel looks great. Trust me when I say that good sales people not only want to make a sale but they know they are going to get referrals. When your new clothes get noticed, you are going to tell people about the wonderful sales person who helped you put your outfit together.

Dressing up doesn't have to mean a suit. It means just looking good. Doing your hair is part of the process. You want to make sure your hair is styled nicely instead of the 'you just woke up' look. Men, make sure your beard is trimmed nicely, and ladies, apply your makeup. You don't have to overdo makeup. Sometimes the eyes and lips will do and say it all.

I have staff members in my business and in my salons that sometimes say: "I don't like to wear makeup." Well that's funny to me because when it's Friday night and they are punching out, they run out to their cars and come back with their best night-clubbing outfit and then they do each other's hair and makeup and they look knock-out gorgeous. I ask them: "Where are you guys going?" and they tell me they are going out dancing. I ask them why they took the time to change their hair style, put makeup on and to dress up. And they reply unequivocally: "It makes us feel great and look great. It's a given rule when you are out at the club you have to look good." Then I wonder to myself why they don't want to look just as beautiful and amazing for their customers.

I remember a client walking into my salon who was immediately drawn to one specific hairstylist. The client pointed at her and said: "I want her to do my hair." I asked why she picked that particular stylist and she said: "Well look at her! Her haircut and color are beautiful not to mention the way she dresses with such flair." The client didn't even wonder about the stylist's actual results with others. She was judged solely on how *she* looked. The better question would have been "*Who* had cut *her* hair?", but because the hairstylist was looking good, the client wanted that – never mind how she got it! The hairstylist didn't cut her own hair – another stylist did it.

We all want to look good and feel sexy. Here is just a little hint: if you decide to go shopping in your pajamas, that is not the time to hand out your business card.

Now that we've talked about looking good, let's talk about standing tall. You own who you are and what you do. Have you ever seen someone enter the building and walk into the room and you wonder: "Who is that?" The person looks important just by the way he or she walks and dresses with confidence and charisma.

When you stand tall and confident, people have a way of seeing you and approaching you much differently. My advice is to manage your present from the future. Have I confused you? Let me explain.

If you sit back and visualize your future "in a positive way," what would it look like, who would you be, where would you live, what would you be driving and how much money would have? How happy would you be? Now that you see your future, you need to start acting that way in the present. I know if you picture that clearly in your mind, you will be standing tall and exuding confidence.

Don't worry that you don't actually have it now because you are going to move closer to it with the power of your belief. It doesn't matter if you are tall or skinny, short or chunky. Here's a great story that I like to tell to show you what I mean.

I witnessed a four foot eleven inch young woman standing up to her six foot five inch boyfriend and setting him straight. You talk about somebody standing confidently. She had one hand on her hip, her chest out and her finger waving in the air. You could just see whatever she was saying was making an impact because all you saw was that six foot five inch guy looking down with his deep voice saying: "I'm sorry, I'm sorry." I observed a four foot eleven inch female who knew what she wanted and knew what she stood for. It felt a little like a David and Goliath story.

What happens if you don't stand tall or confident? That's when the bully typically shows up. I want to show you how to avoid that happening.

There's an exercise I like to use at my seminars. I have two people stand up and they choose who is going to be Partner A and who is going to be Partner B. Partner A is instructed to stand like a despondent person with head down and looking depressed. Partner B is the designated bully. I tell B to push or shove A on the shoulder. As that happens, A practically falls on the floor. When the depressed person is ready the bully shows up.

Then I have A stand up again and I say,

"Stomp your feet on the ground so you feel planted there, standing tall and strong. You are superman or superwoman with a cape flowing off your back!"

Now I repeat this three times or until I feel the person look confident and unstoppable. Then I instruct B to give another shove. When that happens, you can see Partner A can hardly move now. It's almost like a scene from a

Bruce Lee movie. Why? The timid person stood confident and tall. When you stand that way, no one can push you around.

Bullies prey on the not-so-confident or hopeless types because they know their target and who they can push around.

After women experience this exercise, they go out on the street with confidence. A few have reported back telling me,

"Men don't approach me that much and maybe it's because I am looking too intimidating."

Actually it's because they are so confident and that's a great thing. A confident man who appreciates a confident woman will show up sooner or later. So they are doing a good job keeping away the bullies for now.

Imagine getting up every morning and doing what you love every day. It only makes sense to take the time to dress up so you look fabulous. Once you've completed all the finishing touches on hair and face, look in the mirror and say to yourself,

"I am amazing. I am hot. I am beautiful."

And then give yourself two thumbs up.

Remember this thought,

"You can't climb the ladder of success dressed in the costume of failure."

This is one of my favorite quotes from Zig Ziglar. I believe it.

## <u>What To Do</u>

1. Let's start out by cleaning out your closet. Go into your closet and take out all the clothes that make you feel frumpy, make you feel not-so-good about yourself and that don't fit you anymore. Make sure to take out the ones that you say,

   "One day I am going to get back into this."

2. Put those clothes into boxes or bags and give them away to charity, especially if it has been a year or more since wearing something. Only keep the clothes that make you feel great.

3.  Create a plan to replace what you have given away. Set yourself a budget (don't spend all of your money!), and go out maybe once a week to buy yourself a shirt, a pair of pants or whatever you want to replace. And remember there are great sales out there constantly so you don't have to spend a lot of money.

4.  Once you clean out your closet, get rid of clothes and buy something new, here's what you do next. Dress up in one of your new outfits, do your hair and your makeup. I want you to stand tall and go to your mirror and introduce yourself as confident, beautiful and amazing as you are. Look confident and smile!

5.  As a variation, introduce yourself in the mirror but look frumpy and insecure. Understand your hair and clothes can look wonderful but if you look like you have low self-esteem, then all that dressing up is a waste. You don't exert the person you want people to see.

6.  Now try it the opposite way by standing tall, looking confident and brilliant. Which way do you think people will be more drawn to you?

Whenever you walk into a room, always stand straight and walk tall.

Giulio's Gift

Walk through the door of opportunity, STANDING TALL and DRESSED to IMPRESS.

# Unwrapping Your Gift

# Step 6: Your Value Never Depreciates

I do a presentation where I offer the audience a brand new, crispy, fresh $100 bill. With a $100 bill in my hand, I ask,

"Who wants this $100 bill?"

You should see all the hands that go up. Who doesn't want a $100 bill! Then I say,

"Okay, there are too many of you," and I crumple up the $100 bill. Then I ask again,

"Who wants it now?"

I rough it up in my hands. People continue to raise their hands however there are still too many. I throw it to the ground. I step on it, and I inquire,

"Now who wants it?"

People still raise their hand. So I take further action. Not only do I rough it up, throw it to the ground and step on it, but I turn around and make believe I spit on it and stomp on it. Sounds kind of gross, I know. Then I say,

"Okay, who still wants the $100 bill?"

Not everybody wants it now but there are still people who do.

"Wait a minute," I say. "I roughed up this $100 bill up. I threw it to the ground. I stepped on it. I spit and stomped on it. Why do you still want it?"

And the response is,

"It's still worth $100."

One woman stood up and said,

"It's never lost its value, I want it."

My final question is this: Why is it that in life when we get roughed up, thrown to the ground, stepped on or spit on, we think we've lost our value?

You never lose your value. No matter what happened in your past or what you ever did or will do – you are priceless! No one can ever take that away from you.

A man who goes to one of our schools was born without a hand but I don't think he knows he doesn't have a hand. He signed up for beauty school and everyone was calling me frantically asking how he is going to actually cut hair. I met him and he stuck his hand out or where his hand was supposed to be and I shook his "hand" and he introduced himself and told me that he is here to sign up for the barbering program. He immediately told me,

"I forget that I don't have a hand but I will do whatever it takes. I will be the greatest barber."

From that point, I looked at him feeling so inspired and didn't hesitate to tell my staff,

"Sign him up now."

The staff in admissions just looked at me and stated we don't have the means to teach him. I explained to them,

"He doesn't need means. He knows who he is and he knows he is valuable and he is confident."

He could pity himself and never accomplish anything in life but he knows how to enjoy life and have fun. He knows he has value.

I think he can start a whole revolutionary system with cutting with one hand. If you ever meet a barber by the name of Carlos with only one hand, please introduce yourself. He will stick his hand out even though it's not there because that's how confident he is. He is priceless.

I had the pleasure many years ago of meeting Christopher Reeves. Remember Superman? He said to me that he was happier in the wheelchair than he had ever been because he could make a difference to people showing them how to overcome what he had to endure as well as starting more research for spinal traumas. He truly was Superman in my eyes.

## What To Do

When you forget you're priceless, take out a dollar bill, rough it up and throw it on the ground, step on it and spit on it. Then ask yourself if that dollar lost any value? Remember you can always straighten it out and clean it up and it will be a brand new dollar bill again.

No matter what, you are still needed here.

1.  Write down all the important things that you have done:

    _____

    _____

    _____

    _____

    _____


2.  Write down a list of the interesting people you have met:

    _____

    _____

    _____

    _____

    _____

3. Write a list of the valuable things you have yet to achieve:

   _____

   _____

   _____

   _____

   _____

   _____

Now, take out your list of positive thoughts and remember you are priceless. You just need to brush it off and think about what you are going to do differently.

Giulio's Gift

You can't put a price tag on your TRUE SELF WORTH.

## Step 7: Laugh Often

Humor has been an escape for me from everything. I was a clown growing up. I had to make everyone smile because I knew that's what made them feel good. I would be the butt of my own jokes because when they smiled it made me feel good. Sometimes, we just have to look at things and laugh about them.

Laughter is absolutely the best medicine. Watch shows that make you smile. When a trip doesn't go as you planned, sit back and look at the bright side of things. Discuss all the funny things.

That's what happened a couple of years ago when we went to Italy with our neighbors, Henry and Dania Torres. My family and I got to the airport before anyone else and learned that our flight was delayed. Then the ticket agent casually mentioned that we were lucky we weren't on Alitalia because the airline had gone on strike. That got our attention because Henry and Dania were flying with their kids on Alitalia and were planning to meet us in Rome. We were all going on a cruise together from there. This strike meant our friends were going to miss the cruise!

We called them immediately to alert them about the strike and the need to change their flight plans. They were frantic. They managed to get on a different airline, however had to change planes in three different countries to stay on schedule to meet us.

After they went through all that hassle, they discovered that the airline was only on strike for outgoing flights from Rome. The incoming flights were not affected. How mad do you think they were when they found out they could have stayed with their original itinerary and just flown straight through with their original flight plans? There is obviously more to this story as they had to take three different airlines with three different connections, however it would take another book.

Even though that trip was a couple of years ago we still laugh about it whenever we see the Torres' and reminisce about the trip. We found the humor in it and we're the best of friends today.

There is humor in everything. It's all in how you look at it. You have to look at the bright side of things. Of course in any given moment you may feel very angry and very upset at a situation. However you must then stop and think,

"Is it really worth expending all this negative energy?"

I say it isn't. Learn to laugh it off.

## What To Do

Always look on the bright side of things. Turn a negative into a positive. Rent a funny movie or tell a joke to someone. Reflect on something crazy you did that you can now laugh about.

Giulio's Gift

Life is FAR more pleasant when you can LAUGH your way through it.

# Unwrapping Your Gift

# Step 8:  Be a Quitter (and a Loser)

I hear it now. Some of you are saying,

"Wait a minute, you've been telling me not to quit and you've been giving me all these steps to follow. Now you're telling me it's good to be a quitter?"

Let me tell you what I mean by being a quitter. Get rid of destructive habits – quit smoking, quit drinking, quit overeating, quit abusing and **QUIT COMPLAINING!!!**

Now you don't have to quit all these things if they aren't relevant. If you know that any of these things is destructive to your life and is preventing you from reaching your goals – **STOP IT!** If you know that you might develop emphysema, lose some life-giving oxygen or all of your energy – stop smoking! I know it's not going to be easy. In fact, it's going to be very difficult. However, let me tell you something. It wasn't easy to start smoking, was it? I mean, you didn't pick up a cigarette the first day, take a puff and say [coughing and choking],

"Smoking is a great experience; I think I'll start it."

It was painful, sure it was painful however you chose to do it. It's going to be painful to quit, however you've got to do it. If you're drinking too much, your life will be full of problems. You could hurt yourself or someone else like your loved ones and your job. Drinking and using drugs will also affect your judgment as well as your common sense. If you're going out every night you may be avoiding something important. There's a lot of help out there to support you quitting these destructive habits such as AA meetings, doctors, and free clinics. Search the web for clinics and support in your area.

Most of all, quit complaining. People find it easy to complain when they're not successful. They love complaining about their bosses and their co-workers instead of understanding what they need to do to get to where they want to go.

We spend more time complaining about what's not working than focusing on what will be required to make things work. Complaining takes a lot of time and energy and gets you nowhere. It's destructive and hurtful to the people around you. It's unwise to argue – even if the other person is wrong. The important step is to "make it right". Figure out what you need to do to get to the next step. Don't complain, JUST FIND A SOLUTION! That way you'll find yourself achieving goals a lot quicker. Complaining creates blaming which equals zero results. Solutions create results which equals HAPPINESS.

Complaining = Zero results　　　Solutions = Results = HAPPINESS

## What To Do

Admit your discovery and seek help. You have to be accountable in life. Keep seeking solutions – no matter what. Even if you fall off a wagon, you can get back up. In order to get your life back on track, you need to be in control. Keep a diary because doing that allows you to monitor your feelings and keep track of all the situations you should avoid. Do the following:

## Unwrapping Your Gift

1.  Write down two or three things in your life you'd like to change:

    _____

    _____

    _____

2.  Write down what will happen when the changes are made.

    _____

    _____

    _____

3.  Write down who you'll ask for help in making these changes.

    _____

    _____

    _____

4.  Write down your first step.

    _____

    _____

    _____

5.  Write down when you will take that step.

    _____

    _____

    _____

# Step 9: Get in Shape

Don't panic, I am not telling you to get really skinny in order to be successful. For some reason, many people equate this step with dieting. Getting in shape means to start feeling good about yourself. Take the time to go out for a thirty minute walk three times a week.

Listen to me – the first time I tried to go for a walk the farthest I got was my car. That was day one. I went back inside and cracked open a beer. On day two I got to the second car in the driveway. Day number three saw me go to the corner. Next thing you know I was walking a mile! Then I was walking two miles. Apart from getting in shape, the best benefit I found from walking was the quality time that it gave me. All of a sudden, I had time to think. Walking gave me time alone to visualize all the things I wanted to achieve. It gave me time to feel gratitude for all the blessings in my life. I like to say that you can "kill two birds with one stone" when you walk. You use a nice walk to get in shape while thinking about all the possibilities in your life.

Getting in shape also makes you feel energetic. When I go to the gym in the morning, even if it's for a moderate workout, I release all my stress and feel fantastic. I get rid of any anger or anxiety that has built up. I know that many of us often feel overwhelmed with everything that goes on in our lives. These feelings can lead to anxiety or depression if we're not careful because frequently we don't know how to cope with them.

That's because we have a lot of energy bursting to get out, however we don't know where to channel it. To start releasing stress and anxiety, I suggest taking a long walk, jogging on a treadmill or picking up some weights. One of my favorite gym exercises is hitting a punching bag. It's fun to do and helps you both emotionally and physically.

The important thing is to know that you've got to take care of yourself before you take care of anyone else in your life. When you're sitting on an airplane just before take-off they tell you,

"Put the mask on yourself first, then on any child you might be travelling with. If you're traveling with more than one, pick the most promising first! (Just kidding)."

We must take care of ourselves before we can be helpful to others.

## What To Do

Today is about making healthier decisions in your life. Pick just one thing you can do right now. Drink an extra glass of water or walk to the end of your driveway. If you wait there long enough someone might even pick you up and return you to your house! Maybe tomorrow is the day you'll decide to make your lunch instead of buying fast food. Use the money you saved to join a gym.

What one thing can I do RIGHT NOW to improve my health?

_____

_____

_____

Get a workout buddy. Find someone more motivated than you so you have accountability. It will help prevent you from going out for lunch instead of working out. If I say I'm going to meet someone at the gym, I do it because I don't want to disappoint them.

Write down the names of three potential workout buddies:

_____

_____

_____

Now call one of them and make a plan!

Another thing I highly recommend when starting any sort of improvement program is a tracking sheet or journal. Most gyms offer tracking sheets and I've never met a personal trainer who didn't offer one. They understand the power of keeping on top of your progress and your goals.

Don't let it intimidate you because tracking is actually quite easy. You can even ask someone else to type it out for you if you hate writing things down. There are also online programs to help you with your tracking.

Giulio's
Gift

Take good CARE of yourself
so you can be the BEST
you can be.

## Step 10: Wear a Big Smile

Successful people always seem to be smiling. Do you frequently have a big smile on your face? A smile can make people feel good about being around you. Stand firm with a big grin and extend your hand to say,

"Hi, my name is so-and-so, what's yours?"

When you are confident and genuine, you'll see that people are drawn to you. In the course of a conversation, give compliments. Make it sincere with,

"Hey, I love your jacket. That's a nice shirt. That's a great hairstyle. Your eyes are so pretty. Your jewelry looks great with that dress."

Try to give at least one sincere compliment every time you talk to someone. If you can offer more it never hurts.

Smile all the time! Even when you don't feel like it, fake it. When people encounter a successful, happy person, they are pleased to do business with them or enjoy their company. Don't we all want to hang around positive people rather than those who are grouchy or miserable? I can't tell you the number of times that I've heard this statement,

"Giulio, successful people are happy because they've got a lot of money."

No, NO, **NO**! They've got a lot of money because they're happy. So be happy, stand strong, extend that hand, know who you are and give somebody a compliment. Make them feel outstanding!

In order to learn new ways to be more effective in my business, I got a business coach a few years ago. My coach, Lyn Christian, with SoulSalt, Inc., surprised me when she told me I needed an "elevator speech". I wondered why I needed to speak in an elevator. After all, I'm not usually in an elevator when I'm giving a speech! However, that's just what it's *called*. The idea is to think about what important words you would say to someone in the time it takes for an elevator to go up three floors.

In thirty seconds give a short statement about yourself or your business. It is meant to excite people so that they want to learn more about you. Think about what impactful statements you could say about yourself or your business. It's not as easy as you think. You can use your elevator speech as a way to give out your business card so there can be 'follow-up'.

Here is one of my elevator speeches,

"Hello, I'm Giulio Veglio and I'm a visionary freak. I believe in turning possibilities into action no matter what anyone else thinks or says! My mission is to teach people their true potential. I have a business that inspires everyone to be who they are meant to be and to live authentically."

Trust me. By just giving your "elevator speech," you will be surprised by the questions people will ask and the doors that will open for you. Whenever you are giving your elevator speech act confident and wear that big smile.

When you walk always connect with people. Instead of putting your head down, look someone in the eyes and say,

"Hello, how are you?"

You don't have to give your elevator speech, however at least say hello to everyone as they walk by. Be enthusiastic and remember that successful people are always smiling!

## What To Do

I want you to put a large smile on your face, not one of those little curvy ones. Show those teeth and look in the mirror then try to say something negative. Makes you laugh doesn't it? It's hard to offend anyone with a smile on your face. So before you leave the house in the morning, look at yourself with a big smile on your face and tell yourself a bunch of positive thoughts. Every time you leave the house, it's show time.

The second part of this exercise is to do your final mirror check. Remember that results are everything! What's good is poor; what's great is good; let's strive for OUTSTANDING!

Here's your checklist:

1.    I look outstanding.

|  | | | |
|---|---|---|---|
| Hair | _ outstanding | _ great | _ good |
| Make-up | _ outstanding | _ great | _ good |
| Clothes | _ outstanding | _ great | _ good |

2.    I feel outstanding.

3.    I have an elevator speech memorized and ready to go!

4.    I am always smiling.


Write down three things you can do to improve your appearance:

1.  _____

2.  _____

3.  _____

## Step 11: Cleanse Your Mind

Avoid experiences that are going to expose your mind to the wrong things. Television is the number one culprit. Look at the news. Understand that the prevailing attitude at news stations is,

"If it bleeds, it leads."

Why don't they talk about the great things people are doing? Why do they focus on someone who has killed five people? Why don't they talk about somebody that's saved five people or who did something good for the community? Why don't they talk about all the positive things going on in your community?

The other type of television programming that I avoid is the vast assortment of reality shows. Yes, I know that Jerry Springer is intriguing, however we get too caught up in the drama of people's lives and it feeds our own negative thoughts. The more you feed your mind negativity, the more time it takes to de-program that negativity.

When you watch extreme horror movies, what does it do to you on a conscious or sub-conscious level? It puts fear into your mind. Then you start to worry and ask yourself,

"What if that happens to me? What if I have those dreams?"

When you go to sleep at night after watching a horror movie, you start dreaming that Freddy Krueger is chasing *you*. And in your dreams you can't even run or scream. You're yelling however nothing comes out.

Instead, let's feed our minds with programming that offers positive messages. Or better yet, turn off the television and go outside for a bike ride, a walk or a hike. Listen to motivational CDs and read self-help books. Find the right material to help you continually learn and grow. Cleanse your mind of any thought that steels your smile. Replace it with some other thought that recaptures your beautiful smile.

## What To Do

Let's create a checklist:

### Avoid:

Jerry Springer
Negative co-worker

_____

_____

_____

## Add:

Inspirational book or show
Friend for lunch

_____

_____

_____

Write down everything that is negative in your life and avoid those things because they are road blocks! Whether it's a friend, a place you hang out or a bad habit, make it your priority to change. Commit to transforming negatives into positives for thirty to sixty days. Remember, it takes a minimum of twenty-one days to break a habit and sixty to permanently change it. Your objective is to identify problem areas and then divorce yourself from them. Focus on activities that make you feel good and make you laugh.

| Negative Things In My Life | Positive Replacements |
|---|---|
|  |  |
|  |  |
|  |  |
|  |  |
|  |  |
|  |  |
|  |  |
|  |  |
|  |  |
|  |  |

Keep it POSITIVE.
Overstuff your mind with
POSITIVE THOUGHTS,
so there's NO ROOM for the negative.

# Step 12: Listen and Read

When people come up to me and say,

"I need motivation in my life," my immediate response is, "Read books or listen to CDs!"

For some reason, the most frequent excuse I hear for *not* doing that is,

"I don't have enough time."

Well, you can make time! Even if it's only for fifteen minutes at lunch time, reading something inspiring will nourish and fuel your mind for the rest of the day. The easiest thing I can recommend is to listen to motivational CDs while driving. Why not something into your head that's going to inspire you and give you the tools you need to go to the next level?

I'll be honest with you. I used to hate to read. I was definitely one of the worst readers in the world. I could read a page and not comprehend anything. It was easier for me to listen to CDs or watch a DVD. A librarian helped me get on a path to better comprehension by suggesting that I read about things that interested me rather than try to plough through subjects that totally bewildered me. That really helped and I soon came to realize that there's something magical about reading. There are so many great books to get hooked on.

Search for books that interest you. If time becomes a big issue try the Executive Book Summaries. (EBS) They read and condense the best books into eight page summaries of the key points. What I like about the EBS is that they'll send you the information in a PDF file, an MP3 download or a CD. You can get so much useful information from motivational books and CDs. I don't think you can hear a good CD too often. I've listened to some CDs five times and picked up something new each time. I've read some books multiple times. The more you read and listen, the more you'll get excited about where you're going in life. You'll then find yourself achieving the goals you want to achieve.

You may be thinking that I'm offering suggestions you've heard before. Then why aren't you doing them? See, that's the whole thing. We listen to things over and over again and then ignore them. We're looking for the quick fix, the magic pill or the latest innovation. However, there's nothing innovative about this. My goal is to remind you about things you already know and then to follow-through until you see results.

## <u>What To Do</u>

Don't overwhelm yourself by going out and buying a ton of motivational material right now. Start simple. You already have a copy of this book. Read and reread it. Go over the exercises again and again.

Check out the <u>Resource Directory</u> at the back of this book and see if there are titles that interest you. Google words that motivate you or books that you enjoyed in the past.  Suggestions will come up that you might like. If you have an <u>Amazon.com</u> account, look at the recommendations offered there based on your previous purchases. See what you can find.

HINT – My other book, *A Slap on the Back of the Head*

Write down three books you plan to read:

1. _____

2. _____

3. _____

Write down three websites you plan to check:

1. _____

2. _____

3. _____

As you collect books or CDs focus on the ones that are most important to you and review them often. You can't go to the gym once a year and expect to lose weight and stay fit. You can't take one bath a year and expect to stay clean for the rest of your life. If you aren't a big reader then become a big listener. If you're like me, listen to a comedy CD. I like to go to bed smiling and that's what I do.

Giulio's Gift

You can't **GROW** if you don't **KNOW!**

# Unwrapping Your Gift

## Step 13: Use Common Sense

Common sense tells you what's going to happen, what's going to work and what's going to fail. Common sense is like intuition – it's something you have within you right now. The challenge is to listen to it! It is right here, inside you – always has been and always will be. You just have to tap into it. Becoming aware of your common sense isn't easy to do at first – however once you get the hang of it you can trust it to guide you in all of your decisions.

Did you ever have a gut feeling that said,

"This is the right thing to do." or "Whoa, this is a bad idea!"

That intuition, that churning or peaceful feeling speaking to you is actually common sense. It is important to learn to go with it. Common sense is an accurate compass pointing you in the right direction.

Have you ever gone to a bar with a few friends to celebrate? Let's say it's your birthday. You're having fun and enjoying many toasts. At a certain point, you decide to knock off the drinks for the night. However all of a sudden, a friend comes along and says,

"Come on, have another shot. After all, it's your birthday."

Knowing your limits, you think,

"Oh my God, if I have one more shot I'm going to land on the floor. It'll be the end of my night and I'm not going to enjoy it."

However, you let your friend talk you into it while your body tells you not to do it. It's common sense that tells you not to take another drink.

Have you ever walked into an unfamiliar place late at night? As you pass by a dark alley, the hairs on the back of your neck stand up and you get the definite urge to move a lot faster. Your gut tells you there might be danger there. Listen.

When we were building my first salon in New York, there was a construction worker who had a pit bull. There were signs all over his truck that said "Beware of Dog" and he kept the dog with him at the work site.

A salesman came around and decided to "win over" the dog. He had seen the signs. Even though the dog was restrained, he was protective of his owner and growled whenever anyone came close. However, the salesman was determined and approached the dog to pet it and become his "friend".

I don't recall exactly how many stitches the salesman ended up with, however there were many. The dog tore into the guy, ripping his arm to shreds. He later admitted that his gut was telling him to back off, however he ignored it. Talk about biting back!

When your body tells you "no" it's your common sense speaking. Listen to it. I believe in those feelings that constitute common sense. Trust them. Always go with your first instinct. Let your common sense guide you.

## What To Do

Take this quiz and rate your common sense ability.

1. You are waiting to cross a very busy road. You:
   a. Go ahead and cross. Cars will stop, right?
   b. Wait. Eventually the traffic will stop.
   c. *Take the crossover that's right in front of you.*

2. Somebody just gave you $400. Your checking account has $3 in it and your car payment of $380 is due. You:
   a. Go shopping! Woo, it's free money!
   b. Go out for dinner and order steak and lobster with a nice bottle of wine. Worry about your car payment later.
   c. *Deposit the money and pay the bill.*

3. You're out drinking with some friends. You've passed your "stupid" limit and things are out of control. Your old friend Joe shows up and buys a round for everyone. You:
   a. Keep drinking. Free drinks! Get as many as you can!
   b. Have another one, two or three. I mean, why not? You're already past "stupid". May as well go all the way to "obnoxious".
   c. *Call a cab and go home before the room starts spinning.*

4. You're at the beach enjoying the sunshine and you decide to go for a swim. Standing at the edge of the water, you notice circling fins slightly offshore. Sharks!
   a. Go play with the fishes. They are more scared of you than you are of them, right?
   b. Dip in your big toe, however stay near the shore. Those sharks are probably too busy to notice you anyway.
   c. *DO NOT SWIM. Sharks HAVE been known to eat people.*

**If you answered mostly a:** Good luck with that common sense stuff!

**If you answered mostly b:** You could really use some work in this area. You're getting there! Stop and think twice before making decisions.

**If you answered mostly c:** YOU'VE GOT IT! COMMON SENSE ISN'T SO HARD, IS IT? GREAT JOB LISTENING TO YOUR GUT!

## Step 14: Find a Mentor

Put your common sense skills to work now as you think about including a mentor in your life. Mentoring can take many forms. Some examples are an adult serving as a role model for a teenager, a senior executive sharing career advice with an entry- level employee or a leader inspiring hundreds of people. For me, a mentor is someone who will steer you to success either by example or by coaching.

Find someone that you admire, respect and want to be like. I have many mentors including John Paul DeJoria, Anthony Robbins and my mother and father, just to name a few. My list wouldn't be complete without mentioning two of my greatest mentors: my kids Giulio and Stefano. I look at them in amazement. These guys have no fear. They will do anything it takes to get what they want. My son was nine years old when he achieved a goal I wanted all my life and he did it with passion. He wanted to become a black belt in Martial Arts. I only lasted up to green belt however he went all the way. I was in awe. Anything they want to achieve they go after. I'm proud to say that I helped to instill this attitude in their minds because I made it a point to use the steps in this book with both my boys.

I must be doing a good job following my mentors because the biggest compliment I've ever received is when someone told me that I'm just like Tony Robbins. That's okay by me. Look at him – he's incredibly successful. And if someone thinks I'm like Tony it makes me feel like I'm "on top of the world"! If you want to be like Tony, too, I will help you get there.

Before you locate a mentor, identify the characteristics and values of the people you most admire. I always wanted to be like my father because he taught me the importance of setting goals and doing whatever it took to accomplish them. I wanted to be like my mother because she always demonstrated that working hard was the key to getting all our family's needs met. My mother to this day has amazing energy. She's just like the energizer bunny – she keeps going and going and going.

My parents had drive, passion and vision. As I examine their qualities, I see that if they could do it, so can I. There's only one difference between the people you admire and yourself. They had a burning desire to achieve a specific goal and they didn't let anything stop them. You can do that too! Believe that you can do it because you can.

Sometimes we get so caught up in trying to reach our goals that we only focus on what it takes to reach them. We don't spend the time to reach out and give. The moment you get a mentor is the very moment to become one, too. When someone inspires you, it creates an opportunity for you to inspire others. My parents instilled that in me.

Be a mentor by example. Don't be afraid to use these steps with your family, friends or colleagues. The steps are designed to work with anyone. Share these steps with them and watch them achieve their goals.

## What To Do

Write down the names of people you want to emulate and then research those people. What made them successful? Do you have these qualities? If not, what will you need to do to develop them? (Hint: using this book is a fantastic start!)

Name of someone you would like to emulate:

_____

Be yourself however be inspired by your mentor. Understand why that person is successful. If you don't know your chosen mentor personally, search for more information about them on Google. Find out everything that you can. If it's someone you know arrange a time to interview them and ask some relevant questions.

Here are a few to get you started:

Were you scared at any time in your career?

_____

_____

_____

What would you do differently?

_____

_____

_____

Think of the questions you would ask yourself.
Example:

_____

If you had failed, what would you have done differently?

_____

_____

_____

Do your homework and ask yourself questions that will move you forward.

# Step 15: Successful Failures

One of the most common pieces of advice I've received from my mentors is to learn from your successful failures.

So many people have an intense fear of failure. That fear drains their energy. It's important to turn that psychology around by thinking of failures as discoveries. Every failure is success in disguise! Did you know that it's insane to repeat the same failures over and over again expecting a new result?

Let's say you dated someone who made you miserable. Would you date that person over and over again or would you move on and make a better choice? I'm hoping your choice was to move on!

If you've learned what you don't want out of a relationship, you've made a valuable discovery and then new decisions will follow. Even if the new decisions aren't right, you've at least discovered what you don't want. That's when realize that you didn't really fail at that relationship because it made the next one better. That's what I mean by the term "successful failures".

Discovery is how we grow and become better. Most successful people have failed at least once. They didn't let failure stop them because they learned what wasn't working and took a new approach.

I appreciate Thomas Edison's attitude as he embraced his experiments to invent the light bulb. He said,

"I have not failed seven hundred times. I have not failed once. I have succeeded in proving that those seven hundred methods will not work. When I have eliminated all the ways that don't work, I will find the way that will work."

Have you ever watched a baby when he's learning how to walk? I remember when my oldest son was at this stage. He would crawl over to a couch, pull himself up and begin walking all along that couch. When he got to the end of it he fell, bumped his head and started to cry. I'd pick him up, cuddle him and make everything better. As soon as I put him down, he'd head over to the couch again. He'd pull himself up and start back at the end of the couch. However, this time he'd pause, as if thinking about falling down again and then suddenly head back the other way.

Even at that age he knew failure was not an option. He was learning from his discoveries. In life, we are going to have to fall and bump our heads a few times before we understand what is working and what is not. We might have to cry and it might hurt however we have to understand that if we just keep getting back up, we will succeed. In the end, we will get the results we want.

## What To Do

Let's look back now. What have been your three biggest "successful failures"? You may not see the real success just yet, however bear with me. Write down the first things that came to your mind.

1. _____

2. _____

3. _____

Then answer these questions about each failure:

What did I learn?

1. _____

2. _____

3. _____

What would I do differently next time?

1. _____

2. _____

3. _____

How have they changed my life for the better?

1. _____

2. _____

3. _____

What was the success of the failure?

1. _____

2. _____

3. _____

If you haven't learned anything keep going. Nothing happens by chance. Try again, however approach it differently. Bring totally new ideas to the table. Stop approaching it the same way because, remember, that's insanity.

Giulio's Gift

Your greatest DECISIONS come from your greatest EXPERIENCES and your greatest experiences come from your greatest DISCOVERIES.

To fail is to LEARN.

## Step 16: Face Your FEAR

One of the most commonly reported fears is the FEAR of failure. There's even a scientific name for it – *Atychiphobia*. There is something interesting about the word "fear" that you should know. F-E-A-R is simply False Evidence Appearing Real.

Sometimes you set a goal and give it all you've got, however something happens to throw you off. That's because FEAR came knocking at your door. With a frightening whisper in your ear, you hear,

"Hey, what are you doing? What if you fail? What are people going to think of you? Come on, let's play it safe, don't do this. Stay where you are." So you surrender and you let fear win.

I use to go out dancing with one of my friends. I would find myself encouraging him to ask the girl he'd been checking out to dance. He would never take action without drinking first. One night he finally realized that he was afraid of being judged. He was allowing fear to stop him from having fun.

Strangely, after a couple of drinks, I couldn't keep him off the dance floor. It really wasn't the booze that gave him courage, because he had those dance steps in him. However, he thought the alcohol brought out the moves and the emotions so he drank to take away his fears of being judged by others.

Have you ever meet someone who had been drinking too much – moving from being fun to being obnoxious yet thought they had it going on? They went to that extreme because they had fear in their lives they were trying to ignore.

I experienced a lot of fear when I started speaking professionally. I had finally reached my goal and all of a sudden I started having ridiculous thoughts,

"I can't do this. I need to get out of it. Maybe I'll get hurt and break a leg and *that* will give me a good excuse. No, that's too painful. Maybe I'll tell them I have laryngitis."

Look at the stupid things fear brings out in us! I remember the first time I was backstage waiting for my turn to go on. From behind the curtain I saw the audience. I felt a massive dread washing over my body because fear was taking over. I was *allowing* it to take over instead of letting faith take over.

Fear was saying,

"You're no good. These people are going to think you're boring. You have nothing they want to hear."

I'd start talking and think I was boring the audience. I'd see a guy getting up to leave the room. I wanted to yell out,

"Hey, don't go. It'll get better, it'll get better." He might have just been going to the restroom.

When fear took over, my mouth got dry and my lips stuck to my teeth. I was not only boring – I was funny-looking, too!

It's definitely scary standing in front of a bunch of people and keeping their interest. However, as soon as I started acknowledging my purpose and replacing fear with FAITH, I was on a roll.

F  - Fierce

A  - Attitude

I  - In

T  - The

H  - Heart

I knew I had to share my life; especially this knowledge and these tools so that I can help others open the door to success and happiness.

If you know your purpose fear can't stop you. Put faith over fear. It's so much stronger. Know that what you have to offer is awesome and so are you.

## What To Do

Write down a list of your fears.

1. _____

2. _____

3. _____

4. _____

5. _____

Look at each fear. Ask yourself these questions:

What has fear done for me?

 How has it held me back?

When will I let it go? (You'll notice it's probably done nothing for you and it's holding you back).

It's definitely not a friend you want.

Now, next to each fear you've written down, write a word or sentence of faith. What great things can happen if you substitute fear with faith?

Don't let the word "faith" throw you off. I'm not talking about religion. I'm talking about believing in something. Both of the words "faith" and "fear" represent something. You have to choose which one will rule your decisions.

Which will you choose?

| Fear | Faith |
|------|-------|
|      |       |
|      |       |
|      |       |
|      |       |
|      |       |
|      |       |
|      |       |

Understand that you have a lot to offer and a lot to achieve. There's no false evidence that's going to hold you back from getting where you want to go. Replace all your fears with FAITH. Now ask yourself:

"By having FAITH in myself how much more can I achieve, how much stronger will I become, how much more confident will I be?"

# Unwrapping Your Gift

## Step 17:  No More Negativity

One of the biggest aspects of fear is the need to look good in the eyes of others. Eleanor Roosevelt said,

"No one can make you feel inferior without your consent."

Refuse to give anyone that consent. Don't let anybody tell you not to do what you want. Many people have tried to fill my head with defeatist ideas. They would say,

"You're not smart enough. You were never a good student.  You'd be lucky to become a dishwasher."

The day I woke up and refused to listen to negativity towards me was the day my life changed. What I learned was that I must be the one who makes my own decisions, my own destinies and my own thoughts. **<u>No one else can have that power</u>**.

There are always going to be people in your life who don't want you to succeed. **The reason is they haven't read this book yet!!!**

What other people think of us can be a challenge to overcome however what can be even more challenging is what we think of ourselves! Sometimes we are our own worst enemy and say the extremely negative things to ourselves. We say things to ourselves that we would never say to anyone else.

Even worse, if someone compliments us by saying,

"You look outstanding," our first reaction is,

"No I don't," as if you don't deserve to hear that praise.

Of course, some of us will respond that way just to hear more compliments. That way, you can hear the compliment, over and over.

"Yes you are deserving of that compliment."

Stop it and just take the compliment! If someone says you look really good say,

"Thank you! I feel great, too!"

Speak the positive words, not only in your mind, however out loud as well.

When people used to criticize me, there were a couple of sayings that I inwardly repeated to keep myself positive. One was,

"I can do anything through Christ who strengthens me." The other was,

"I am a mountain. I am strong".

Someone taught me those sayings and they really helped me overcome a lot of negativity in my life. Every time someone told me something negative, or my mind shifted to a negative thought, I would repeat these positive sayings over and over again until the negative thoughts disappeared.

## What To Do

Let's go back to the exercise you did for positive thoughts. Keep a copy of your list of positive thoughts with you all of the time. When someone puts you down take out these thoughts and remind yourself who you are.

If someone says something negative to you once, say something positive to yourself at least three times.

Another thing you can do is to look in the mirror and say,

*"I am smart. I am beautiful. I am intelligent. I can do anything I want to do. I can do anything through Christ who strengthens me. I'm a mountain. I am strong. Nothing can move me. I am invincible. I can achieve anything."*

You can also talk to yourself in the car while you are driving. Tell yourself how wonderful you are! Everybody wears headsets now so anyone who sees you will think you're talking to someone when you're actually talking to yourself. Tell yourself how wonderful you are, how outstanding you are, how generous you are and how giving you are. Tell yourself you can achieve any goal you choose.

Nothing is more inspiring that loving yourself. Here are a few other suggestions. They may sound corny, however try them anyway.

Send yourself a card that says,

"Just because...you're outstanding."

Bake yourself a cake!

Send yourself flowers when you achieve a goal. Don't wait for others to congratulate you because there are people out there who are not going to be happy for you. First, you have to be happy for yourself!

What other ideas do you have?

_____

_____

_____

_____

You BECOME the exact person that you THINK you are.

## Step 18: Focus on Your Good Qualities

I once did an exercise during a speech where I asked the audience to come up with ten things that they wished they could change about themselves. Boy, did the chatter begin! Nobody had a hard time telling the person next to them negative things about themselves.

The hard part came next when I asked them to come up with ten things that are great about themselves. People started slowly, not really sure how their "lists" would be perceived by strangers. Maybe they were afraid to appear conceited or to be judged in other ways. If you want to experience the power of being positive, you've got to focus on your good qualities, both inside and out.

I find that it's easier to start "self talk" with statements like,

"I'm a great person. I go the extra mile. I inspire people. I'm a great mother or father or employee or boss."

Some people think it's cocky to act with confidence, however there's a difference between being cocky and being confident. Cocky people say how great they are. Confident people demonstrate actions and attitudes that are in alignment with the words they speak. Poise and confidence are revealed in their actions. They know their own true qualities and it shows.

I used to focus on other people's qualities much more than my own. I would tell myself that someone else was better at the job than me, etc. Now I realize that I did have real value as a person way back then and at all times. I just didn't see it.

Recently, I was having dinner with a few friends and the conversation turned to our high school days. We started asking questions about one another. Someone asked,

"What do you remember that was bad about Giulio?" and the unanimous response was,

"Nothing, he was always nice and respectful."

Back then I didn't think I was good enough for anything – except being a good friend. I didn't realize how many people had seen that in me until that dinner some thirty years later. Thanks to friends like Lynne, Roselie, Michele and Jean I understood even then that I had some great qualities. Today, I know what those qualities are and I focus on them. I wish I had known that a long time ago because the more I focused on my bad qualities, the more I associated with the wrong people. What you focus on is what you create. Know your qualities and all the great things you have to offer. Then use them as a foundation to build on.

## What To Do

Write down a list of all of your negative qualities. For every negative thing you write about yourself, write three positive things. Fill up as many pages as you can and cross the negative qualities out. Look at the list every morning so you can remember all the good things about yourself. Don't worry about anyone else. Just think about all the good things you have to offer.

While this exercise is similar to other exercises, it's different in that these are thoughts that YOU have about YOURSELF! When you are writing the positive replacements, be sure to focus on the BENEFITS of every positive quality.

Negative

1. _____
2. _____
3. _____

Positive

1. _____
2. _____
3. _____

Giulio's Gift

FOCUS on everything that is POSITIVE about yourself and build upon those qualities.

# Unwrapping Your Gift

# Step 19: Look Yourself in the Eyes

If you can look yourself squarely in the eyes you'll be able to face other people with confidence and self-assurance. Start by looking at yourself in the mirror. Look into your own eyes every day and tell yourself what a fantastic person you are... you are a versatile cook, a creative artist, a dedicated worker, a loving mom, a caring dad or whatever fits. You can then face other people and they will immediately sense your positive qualities without you having to say a word.

Do you know how many people can't face themselves because they're disgusted by what they see? Trust me, I know.

For many years the low self-esteem that was with me every day was obvious every time I looked in the mirror. Behind my eyes I could see disappointment with my past actions and my inability to live up to my potential.

Most of us have been fed with so much negativity that it's hard to face ourselves and contemplate these things. When you start looking at yourself in a whole different way, you'll become confident and this will impact how others see you. However, if you look at yourself in the mirror and put yourself down by telling yourself you're ugly, fat or unsuccessful – you'll create your own failures.

I'm not saying you have to be conceited! Conceited is when you walk up to somebody and say,

"Hey, I'm great."

Confidence is when you can look at yourself and say,

"I'm great." – Then others will see it in your nonverbal actions.

Look at yourself every day in the mirror and tell yourself how outstanding you are and how you can achieve anything you want with the faith that you have, with the abilities you have, and with the gifts you've been given. Don't tell me who you are, SHOW ME! Your nonverbal actions will always speak louder than your words.

## What To Do

I want you to look straight into the mirror and think about how great you look and how fantastic you feel. I want you to practice this every time you pass a mirror. I know you're saying,

"C'mon Giulio, this is ridiculous."

However, this is what successful people do. When they look in the mirror they don't see failure. They see success because they give themselves positive reinforcement and really mean it.  That's what it takes to be successful. When you believe it, other people will see the energy in your eyes and believe it too!

Giulio's Gift

The most significant thing you can do is to FACE yourself and BELIEVE in the POWER of YOU.

# Unwrapping Your Gift

## Step 20: Carry on a Conversation with Yourself

Have you noticed lately that people walk down the street talking and you can't tell if they're talking on the phone or talking to themselves? What do you think about the idea of talking to yourself? Is it okay or will people think you're crazy? Personally, I think it's perfectly fine to talk to yourself as long as you don't catch yourself saying,

"Huh? Who said that?!!"

If you're thinking right now, you're talking to yourself. When you debate two sides of a challenge in your mind, you're talking to yourself. Everybody does this. We all have little debates with ourselves and we constantly engage in self-talk. Sometimes it takes place in our minds, however sometimes it happens out loud as we visualize and rehearse talking to a specific person or persons. I talk to myself in the morning and say,

"You should get out of bed and work out. No you shouldn't, it's too cold right now!"

Sometimes I win, sometimes I lose. Sometimes my thoughts argue with each other, inspire each other or soothe and comfort each other. I entertain myself all the time. Hold on, I'm getting a standing ovation right now and I'm taking a bow. Thoughts can be very powerful and I'm always the star of my own thoughts.

In my first book, *A Slap in the Back of the Head*, I introduced my alter egos – Sonny and Vin. I talked to them when I needed to "dump" on someone or to process my feelings. They represented an outlet for my self-talk. If I was at a party with friends who wanted to keep drinking all night, Sonny would encourage me,

"Go for it, have fun with your friends." Vin would have emphatically told me,

"You've had enough. Go home."

Talking to yourself is normal. We do it every second that we're not talking to someone else. Thinking is talking to yourself. Meditating is talking to yourself. Singing inside your head is serenading yourself.

You might be visualizing that you're singing to a hundred people while your eyes are open as you walk down the street – taking a bow and telling yourself,

"That wasn't bad. You're a pretty good singer."

How you talk to yourself can be triggered by the day's events. You can convince yourself to believe that you have to be angry, mad, upset or assertive. **This can create self-talk that leads to bad decisions or ugly nonverbal facial expressions. In fact, your face reflects your self-talk!**

Talk yourself out of negative moods and think of reasons why you should not be angry or say those nasty things on the tip of your tongue. Be good to yourself and make sure that your self-talk is building on your good qualities instead of emphasizing the ones that bug you. Now your nonverbal expressions will be so much sweeter, making you more approachable.

Talking to yourself and convincing yourself how wonderful you are will attract people to you. They'll see the positive attitude written all over your face. On the other hand, if you're angry on the inside, people won't approach you because they'll see your negative body language. What's wrong with your face? What are you bitter about? Sometimes people will watch you laughing at yourself because you told a funny joke when no one else was around. This sparks an interest in what just happened because they want to laugh as well.

**Self-talk is for you and nobody else. It's your best friend. You can tell it what you want and it won't reveal anything to others. You can share your darkest secrets or your greatest successes and it won't get jealous, angry or mad. It'll be happy and cheer you on. Some people call this their inner spirit or "angel". It's a great tool you can always rely on when you really need the support.**

## What To Do

Think of something positive to say to yourself and "anchor" it into your consciousness by attaching a physical movement to it. Pick an anchor such as touching your shoulder or slapping your hands as you repeat the positive thought. This will create a key connection for you and "cement" the words into your mind. For example, an affirmation I regularly use is,

"I'm a mountain, I am strong, I can overcome anything."

Each time I say it, I hold my head high and pound my chest with my fist. People might wonder what's going on when I do it, however that's okay. *I* know why I do it and that's all that matters.

This particular anchor has become secondary to me. Often when I need to lift myself up, I just pound my chest and get immediate effects. This demonstrates the incredible power of positive self-talk. Creating the physical anchor to go with it actually magnifies the power. That's why it's critical *not* to give your negative thoughts an anchor.

Giulio's
Gift

Talk to yourself with
POSTIVE thoughts and
TRUST what you say.

# Step 21: Mind Your Manners

Once you learn how to respect yourself it's a lot easier to respect others. One of the best ways to demonstrate respect is to exhibit good manners. You probably heard this growing up –

"Mind your manners, over and over!"

My parents insisted that their children use good manners at all times. I can show you the belt my father used to teach me those manners! At first I couldn't understand why my father was always slapping me on the back of the head for holding the fork wrong or not sitting up straight. I thought he was too picky. However, now when I go out with people who don't have manners, I can see why my dad was hard on us about etiquette. Have you ever watched someone who doesn't know how to hold a knife and fork while cutting? Or even worse, someone who uses his hands to eat meat then sucks loudly on his fingers to get the seasoning off every finger! Even writing about it grosses me out.

When you're in a job interview or out with company, people observe your manners to see if they want to associate with you. Remember, as you're trying to further yourself in life, people are watching you. Hopefully, you wouldn't burp at the table or yell profanities at your kids to get them to be quiet. When I see others doing this, I'm more embarrassed for them than they are for themselves!

It's human nature to watch other people and judge their actions. The way you behave helps to define your character. You might say that you only act poorly at home however there might come a time when you're so used to performing bad manners at home that you carry the practice into the outside world unconsciously. The more you act a certain way, the more those actions become habits.

With my own sons I stress respect, integrity and good manners. I do this by example not with a belt. I model the process and explain why manners are important. It's effortless to show good manners. Shake hands when meeting someone new. Say,

"No thank you" not "Nope", and "Yes, thank you," not "Yep."

Don't address a stranger,

"Hey, dude," especially if the stranger is female.

Be sure you don't let technology force you into rude habits. I was recently at a top hotel checking in and the young lady at the front desk was very polite. However all of a sudden, her cell phone went off to alert her of a personal text message and she was so attached to her phone that I could tell she was "itching" to read it. It got so bad that she told me she would get fired if she didn't turn it off. However, when she went to shut it down, she was struggling extremely hard to look at the text message – as if she simply could not survive without reading it. This is an example of how modern devices can impact our natural human impulse to consider the needs of those around us.

Today, everywhere we go people are texting on their phones. It's hard to have to face to face conversations and it's disrespectful to others who are with you. Let's put the technology away for a while and get back to human interaction. The only time it's ok to have a phone out is if you have kids sick at home and need to be on call.

Other ways to show good manners include holding the door for people walking behind you and attentively looking at people when they're talking to you. Manners are something we display by acting with confidence. Conversely, successful people always display great manners.

## **What To Do**

Come up with ways that manners are important to you, as well as some you feel you need to work on. Write down some of the ways you can improve your manners and what good manners actually mean to you. Get on the internet and research table manners and nonverbal manners. Think of ways to you can integrate more good manners into your life.

What websites did I visit regarding manners?

_____

_____

_____

What did I learn from those websites?

_____

_____

_____

As you look around during your daily life, take note of those who don't have good manners. How do they look to you?

_____

_____

_____

**Unwrapping Your Gift**

What would others say about my manners?

_____

_____

_____

How can I improve my manners and how would it benefit me if I did?

_____

_____

_____

Giulio's Gift

It's not what you think but how you ACT. Always show RESPECT for others and respect will be YOURS.

## Step 22: Control Your Emotions

Emotions have a tendency to get in the way of making the right decisions. For instance, at work you may hear one side of a story and get angry. This provokes you to start gossiping and compose a nasty email. Before you think it through clearly, you hit the "send" button, only to realize the next morning,

"Oh my God, what have I done?

If you let your feelings dictate your actions you may lose sight of your intentions and your goals. It's very hard to retract something you said in anger. I have an "Italian" temper. I'll explode for five minutes and when *that* happens it's like a nuclear bomb going off. However, after the five minutes are up, I'll ask you to go get an ice cream. However, even though *I* get over it very quickly the other person often remains REALLY upset.

When your emotions are running wild, let the "ink dry". Don't make any rash decisions. Think about it and let it set in for a day or two. When your emotions are at a "ten" on the anger scale, just wait – tomorrow they're probably going to be at a "three".

There have been times when I've become emotionally involved with disputes that had nothing to do with me. At those times, I failed to disassociate myself.

Once there was a person at work who came in and started ranting and raving at Joe, a co-worker. Joe used information from the "grapevine" to drive Lisa, his co-worker, crazy! Her feelings were so hurt that she requested a meeting with the managers and Joe to diffuse the situation. She came into the meeting in "freak-out" mode, screaming and swearing. Joe just sat there, calm as can be. In the end, he came out smelling like a rose. Who was going to believe that *he* caused the uproar when *she* was so "out of control" at the meeting?

Whether it's in your personal affairs or your business, be a good listener and take it all in calmly. Be patient! Then call a friend and ask him to rant and rave while you share your story. Choose a loyal friend who will keep your confidence and reinforce your common sense. **Better yet, think it out within yourself.**

One of the tricks I use is to sit down and write out the points I want to make before going into a meeting or sending an email. Gathering your thoughts and emotions show that you have respect for others and present yourself in a professional and ethical way. I sometimes still have work to do on this matter – no one is perfect. However, I am working on controlling my Italian temper.

## What To Do

When anything comes up that triggers you, take time to back away. Here are some ideas to try:

1. Say, "I need to calm down before I respond." (Ask for thirty minutes or even the rest of the day.)

2. Hold your emotions in check and write down what you are feeling *before* you respond.

3. Ask yourself if this is the fight you want to pick. Sometimes you have every right to be angry however, in the end, you need to understand the outcome you really want.

Always remember that anything you write or say can haunt you for years to come. Make sure that what you actually write is something you want to share with the entire "cyber-world". Once your words appear online they can be seen for a very long time. A good "rule of thumb" is to write your message on paper first – then let the ink dry. Reread it the next day *before* sending it. You may then want to change your approach to get more effective results.

One last thing, if you do lose yourself, just remember to say,

"I'm sorry, that's not who I am or what I do. I hope you can forgive me and we can move forward to a healthier relationship."

# Unwrapping Your Gift

## Step 23: Love Everyone

Even though you know what your goals are, there may be people who want to prevent you from achieving them. Some block you from getting there because they don't want to be left behind. Remember – it's not their goal and they're full of fear. They wouldn't think of doing what you are, so how do you deal with them?

Understand their thoughts and actions and forgive them. Love them for who they are.

One of my goals was to open Paul Mitchell Schools. When I shared this goal, many people thought I was crazy. I heard all kinds of criticism,

"You're risking too much money. You don't have the money to lose. What if it fails?"

When they found out I was leaving New York to start my first school in Orlando, they reacted even more negatively,

"Are you crazy? You'll fail and end up in the street with no support."

I was sharing my plans with the wrong people. As a result, they almost had me doubting myself. Why share our goals with them? Why not share them with people who will encourage us to get where we want to go? Know who your enemies are and who will try to prevent you from getting where you want to go. They only act out of jealousy or fear.

However, don't stop loving them because they don't really mean to be negative. Hopefully you will share this book with them to help them on *their* way. Successful people give love to those who need it the most! If they ask why you're not sharing your goals with them, help them to understand that you love them, however don't support their negativity.

## What To Do

Your goals are going to be different from those of others. Know who to share your goals with. Recognize who your enemies are – those who try to prevent you from reaching your goals. Share with those who can support you.

Compile a list of friends who support you and spend more time with them. Don't keep track of your enemies and the wrongs they have created because that will turn you toward the negative aspects of things. It *is* wise to develop the ability to recognize them so you can fill your life with positive people who inspire you. However, do continue to love them from a distance.

Giulio's Gift

LOVE your enemies and CELEBRATE with your amazing friends.

# Step 24: Give More of Yourself

If someone says,

"Could you help me clean up my area? I'm really falling behind," answer,

"Of course!"

If you know what they need – do it, even if you think they would never return the favor. Successful people give more and "go the extra mile".

In 1937, Napoleon Hill wrote, in his timeless bestseller, *Think and Grow Rich,* about Andrew Carnegie's discovery of a young worker by the name of Charles M. Schwab. Mr. Schwab started at Carnegie's steel mill in 1901 as a day laborer and worked his way up to President of the U.S. Steel Corporation due to his willingness to go the extra mile, combined with his positive attitude. These attributes also netted him as much as $1 million in bonuses to add to his annual salary of $75K. By today's standards, that would be a $1.5 million salary with a $15 million bonus!

As Mr. Schwab exhibited over one hundred years ago, it really does pay to go the extra mile. Even if you don't get a million dollar bonus, it'll make you *feel* like a million dollars. Imagine what it does for the recipient! How would you feel if every time you asked for a little help you got a *lot*? What if someone saw you needed something done and just went ahead and did it? It would most definitely make you feel really valued.

You've probably seen the bumper sticker that says,

"Practice random acts of kindness."

I think acts of kindness should be practiced on a regular basis rather than "at random"!

## What To Do

`Remember, true "giving" means expecting nothing in return. If they are mad, it's a contract, not a gift!

Take out your notebook and write down the names of three people you are going to help over the next three days.

1. _____

2. _____

3. _____

Now, brainstorm ideas about how you can go the extra mile for each one of them. As you do this remember – no idea is a dumb idea. Write down everything that comes to your mind. You'll be surprised how ideas that seem "dumb" to begin with spawn thoughts that become brilliant notions to build on. Be flexible. As you go through the next three days with the intention of helping those people, look for *other* people you can support and other ways you can help the people that you're already helping.

When you get home tonight, instead of making the usual beeline to the kitchen to stuff your face, or to the sofa to catch up on the latest shows – look around. What could you do that to help out? Take a few minutes to give more of yourself

Pick someone at work and do something special for them. It can even be the janitor or the receptionist. Maybe bring them lunch or just volunteer,

"Is there anything I can do to make your day better?"

Do it with a big smile on your face!

*Giulio's Gift*

**Relationships are never temporary. They IMPACT your life FOREVER.**

# Unwrapping Your Gift

# Step 25: Honor Every Relationship

Successful people work most on relation-ships with their friends, family and colleagues. Keep strong relation-ships with people who support you and your goals. Relationships are very easy to make and very easy to break. Value the ones that are built around honesty, love and trust. The best way I can describe an ideal relationship is when I talk about the one with my sons. If you have never experienced what unconditional love is, have a child! My sons don't care how short or tall I am, or how rich or poor. They demonstrate true love and that love is something I will never allow myself to lose. Their unconditional acceptance helps my self-esteem on a daily basis.

I have known people who let a trivial fight with their parents get in the way of having an ongoing relationship. When one of the parents dies, it creates an enormous sense of guilt that should never have been. It makes carrying on with the other parent somewhat difficult. I've also seen those who had no relationship with a parent experience their death with a great deal of regret – to the point where they never got over it. Don't let it be too late for you. Whether personal or professional, relationships are critical to your success.

## What To Do

1. Think of all your great relationships and write them down.
2. Discern whether they are genuine or need improvement. Then look at your list again and make a note beside any that need work.
3. Make sure that those relationships that are *really great* stay that way and most importantly, which ones are not – but need to be.
4. Are there people that you can send a quick note to? (To show that you care.)

1. _____  \_\_\_genuine \_\_\_fake \_\_\_good \_\_\_\_needs work

2. _____  \_\_\_genuine \_\_\_fake \_\_\_good \_\_\_\_needs work

3. _____  \_\_\_genuine \_\_\_fake \_\_\_good \_\_\_\_needs work

4. _____  \_\_\_genuine \_\_\_fake \_\_\_good \_\_\_\_needs work

5. _____  \_\_\_genuine \_\_\_fake \_\_\_good \_\_\_\_needs work

Indicate how you will create great relationships with the ones you want to improve. Start by reaching out – call these people to catch up. Re-awaken your relationship.

If you have any family relationships that are broken, **fix them!** Don't let your emotions get in the way. Show the initiative to heal them.

Take the time to tell each one of them,

"I feel there has been a communication breakdown between us. If I did anything to offend you, I am sorry. I'd like to put all of that aside and renew our relationship. I value you as a person. I don't want to have any regrets later on by not telling you how much I care about you today".

# Unwrapping Your Gift

# Step 26:  Hang With The Best

Hang out with people who motivate you. If your goal is to lose weight, would you go to the gym with someone who is in worse shape than you? I've gone to the gym with a friend who likes to go through the motions of a work out. Once we get inside the gym and talk for a few minutes he says,

"I'm hungry, are you?"

Of course, I say,

"Yeah, let's go eat."

He doesn't motivate me and I obviously I don't motivate him. I get a "heart-stopping grand slam" breakfast instead of a "heart-happy" workout.

Then I ended up going to the gym with a friend who loved working out. That was his passion!  When we got together we got a lot accomplished and I ended up feeling totally energized and motivated.

Not only did he motivate me, I motivated him. This was much better for both our hearts!

I have many friends that inspire me. When we are together we don't dwell on negative things. We don't have time. We motivate each other to achieve our goals. We've created a great support network for each other. I love associating with those that empower me. These days, if I run into someone who is negative – I walk away. Who wants to hang out with negative people? Who wants to get constantly dragged down? I know what that feels like because I used to associate with types like that in the past. I once caught myself in Las Vegas with a friend, who was being very negative and said to me,

"Wait a minute. I've got to go to the restroom, I'll be right back."

Thirty minutes later he wasn't back. An hour later he still wasn't back. I started walking around and discovered him with a bunch of other people having a great time. He caught me out of the corner of the eye and said,

"Oh, man! Listen, I got caught up and forgot about you waiting."

That's when it occurred to me – no one likes to hang out with negative people. Associate with fun, motivated people and strive to support them as they work to believe in themselves. Motivate them, encourage them and show them you believe in them so they can really get where they want to go!

## **What To Do**

Think about the positive people in your life. Who motivates you or inspires you? Write down the first three names that come to mind: (make a list for them)

1. _____

2. _____

3. _____

As you write these names, notice your reactions to the thought of them. Do they bring a smile to your face? If so, you're on the right track. If not, then realize that these are not the people you want to spend time with.

Sometimes, we think we *should* want to spend time with someone when they may not be the best choice for us. Maybe they are the right choice for someone else, however if there's any negativity associated with them, listen to your intuition and say,

"Not right now."

Think of ways you can spend more time with positive people. Hang around them more, go out to dinner with them more and talk to them more. Keep this list close at hand because if you stay positive, motivated people will surround you.

However, be careful not to resort to stalking them. Be sincere and receptive to their needs. Understand that they may not be completely open to spending more time with you for whatever reason. If this is the case, find someone else and move on.

Look for people who are always excited and ready to get things moving. This will make you excited to be around them and want to do what they are doing. I love to be around people who make coffee nervous because they are so excited and full of energy. Always hang with the best.

Giulio's Gift

Tell me who you HANG with and I'll tell you WHO you are.

# Unwrapping Your Gift

# Step 27: Make Deliberate Choices

Everything in life is a choice. You choose to drink too much or to smoke too much. You choose whether you're going to take action or sit down and stay quiet. You choose to use your common sense or let fear win. All choices have consequences. When faced with a decision, some of the questions you might ask yourself include,

"Should I do this? Is it ethical? If I get caught what will happen?"

If you get caught, you have no one to blame but yourself. You made the choice.

I made a choice to smoke when I was younger. No one made me do it. Even though I had friends pushing it on me, however I made the final choice. Don't blame others for wrong choices, own it and understand that you can choose to change your choice anytime you want. I did. I chose to stop smoking many years ago. It was painful; however I'm glad I did. Just because we make bad choices doesn't mean we can't change them.

Everything in your life is about the choices you make. My advice is to always choose to be your best. You can choose not to do any of the exercises in this book and then say you didn't benefit from it. On the other hand, you can choose to do them and learn how to achieve happiness. You choose your destiny.

## What To Do

This is an exercise of contemplation. You don't need to write anything down.

The next time you are faced with a decision say,

"I choose to do this." Or, "I choose not to do this"

Imagine the outcomes before they happen and decide which ones you willing to own. Say to yourself,

"What I'm about to do is my choice. The results are my responsibility..."

I know you will make the right choices in the end even when you made the wrong choices in the beginning.

Give up or fight.
Be happy or miserable.
It's YOUR CHOICE.

## Step 28: Stay Focused

Have you ever met anyone who is so focused on what everyone else is doing that he doesn't get anything done for him-self? This tends to happen when we start to feel overwhelmed. We start avoiding what we need to do by getting involved in what other people are doing.

When you are too consumed with someone else's life you have no time to focus on what *you* need to do to meet your goals. Instead of focusing on improving your quality of life and staying away from unnecessary negativity, you focus on too many time-wasters such as reality TV, video games or internet surfing. The usual cause for this is either boredom or procrastination.

I understand how it can happen. If I'm flipping through the channels I can easily stop and get caught up in a show I wouldn't normally watch. My life may be messy at times, however I can always find someone on TV whose life is worse.

In the workplace, instead of focusing on your career and what you want to achieve, many times you are worried about what your co-workers are doing and how much money they are making or who they are sleeping with. Who cares? Are you bored or jealous? Do you have too much time on your hands? Focus on your path instead of someone else's. Why would you let what other people are doing affect what you are doing?

In order to have better quality experiences you have to be present in the moment, both mentally and physically. When you're working focus completely on the task at hand. When you're at home, avoid anything that takes you away from your family and friends. You don't need someone else's problems. We all need to focus on the important people in our lives and the key challenges that we face. The best way to do so is by being completely present to our own experience.

I've learned that our mind can only focus on one thing at a time and we always draw closer to what we focus on.

We create our own successes by what we pay attention to, what we experience and what we use our energy for. Be in the moment. Stay focused. Avoid anyone or anything that fades you away from your true focus.

## What To Do

Before you start your day, focus on being the best you can be in the situations that will arise. Take a moment to visualize the right thoughts. For example think,

"I'm at home and I'm going to have a nice healthy breakfast with my family."

When I leave home, my mind shifts to where I need to be next – work. While I'm there I focus on what my task is *in each moment*. You can empower yourself by doing the same. Review your career path and your opportunities. If you aren't sure, meet with your manager and ask him how you can advance your career path. Today is the best day to focus on yourself, your health and your well-being. Write down your focus for the day.

_____

_____

_____

_____

Giulio's Gift

What you FOCUS on is what you GET.

# Step 29: Visualize Your Dream

One of the best ways to set your focus for the day is to spend some time visualizing each morning. Close your eyes and picture yourself in a successful future. See your-self in the middle of your created success such as speaking in front of people or opening a business – it doesn't matter as long as it involves your true vision of success towards happiness.

Before I opened my own salon and school, I visualized what it would look like and what the employees and customers would look like. I visualized every detail – as it if were actually happening!

The key is to visualize that your dream has already been accomplished. Before I do a seminar, I visualize the audience enjoying the information. Then I picture individuals coming up to me afterwards telling me about some aspect of my presentation that made a difference for them. I take it further by seeing these people using what I presented to achieve their own successes.

You visualize all the time without even realizing it. When you're in your car and crank up the radio, it's not because you like loud music. It's because you visualize yourself on stage performing the concert. You visualize the crowd going nuts until another car pulls up. Then you become a ventriloquist, right? All of a sudden you start singing under your breath, and you start edging your car up a bit so you can go back into that singing visualization.

Hey, rock away! If singing in front of people is your dream, don't let anybody stop you. They might look at you and say,

"What an idiot." Or, "They're crazy."

Refuse to accept that insult and have fun.

Visualization is a powerful tool however you will also need action to make it work. I know this is true because I visualized losing weight every day however didn't lose a pound until I went to the gym and started working out. Visualization is just a dream until you add the action steps that will make it a reality.

## What To Do

1. Before you start the day, sit down and visualize all the positive things that are going to happen that day.

2. Visualize every detail clearly.

3. Write down all the steps it's going to take to make them happen and how you are going to put these steps into action.

Giulio's Gift

See your GOALS and DREAMS playing in your mind like a movie. Then take ACTION.

## Step 30:  Live Your Dreams

One of my dreams was to be successful. It was hard for me to figure out what that really meant because I always thought I was a failure. I was unable to move forward until I truly believed I could attain the dreams I dared to dream.

All I knew was that I had a gift for business and teaching and I wanted to open a school. I didn't have every detail formulated at the beginning however I did have the vision. Before my vision was believable, all I could do was stand outside at night, stare at the sky and dream of moving to Florida and opening my business. My family kept asking,

"What are you doing out there?"

When I finally shared my dream with them, you should have seen their eyes. They wanted to be supportive however they were scared for me.

Once I realized that it was okay to have a dream and not be afraid of failure, I took the plunge. Remember the principle of successful failures? You have to have the will and the strength.

I believe that if you want something badly enough, you can make it happen. You don't know unless you try. I am proud that I followed my dreams and visions because they were successful ten-fold.

My parents helped me believe in dreams. They moved to America to give their kids a better life. It was a "do or die" situation. If it didn't work they would have had to go back to Italy. However they persisted – paid off their house, bought a car and made plans for their children's future. They didn't stop to think about the consequences – they just kept focusing on the dream.

Live your dreams and add actions to them and your dreams will never stop. Just follow the line from the song, "Somewhere Over the Rainbow",

"The dreams that you dare to dream really do come true."

## What To Do

Let's get a little risky.

1. Write down your ultimate dream. Now put a time limit on it.

2. Write down why you want to follow this dream and what the benefits will be. It can be anything from moving to another country to taking a new job or starting a family.

3. Write down the action steps you will take to make this happen. Go and do it!

Now I want you to write me and share your dream with any and everyone who will support you. www.Visionaryfreak.com

# MAKE IT HAPPEN

Now that you have finished this book, you know far more about yourself. You have identified what your positive and negative belief systems are and how they define you. As a result, you've started focusing more on your positive beliefs. You're never going to let negative thinking impact your life again. Even if these thoughts come back to haunt you, you're going to throw them out.

Now I turn it over to you. Let the following words serve as an affirmation to you. Whenever you feel you need a boost, come back and read this aloud as often as possible.

*I'm not going to procrastinate because that's what causes fear, anxiety, laziness and pain. I'm going to finish what I start because that's what gives me a sense of accomplishment and a feeling of success. I won't accept or believe insults.*

*I'm not going to listen to anything negative. I'm not going to let other people's ideas get in the way of my success. I know I can achieve anything I want. I'm moving forward.*

*I'm priceless – no matter what. I know I can't change my past however I can change my future. No matter how much I've been roughed up in the past, thrown to the ground or stepped on, I'm worth every single penny. I never lost my value.*

*Each day, I get up, feel good about myself and dress up. I feel like a billion dollars. I dress like the successful person that I am.*

*I have mentors in my life. I'm like them. I believe that if they can do it, I can do it. I'm a mentor to others and I share my success.*

*I have a sense of humor. I laugh about things I've done and about discoveries I've made in my life. I crack up when I think about the stupid little things that happened along the way. Even though those things are now gone, it's okay to laugh about them.*

*In order to reach my goals, I visualize them every day. I see myself succeeding. I see people cheering me on and supporting me all the way.*

*I smile no matter what room I walk into. I always have the biggest smile on my face because I am a success. I am fantastic! My life is great in this moment.*

*When someone asks me for help, I don't hesitate to go the extra mile.*

*I've stopped all the destructive habits in my life. I quit those things because they're not healthy and they no longer align with the life I want to live.*

*I know who my enemies are so that when I'm sharing my goals, I share them with the people who will support me. I associate with the best.*

*I know my good qualities and I am constantly building upon them. I listen to motivational CDs and read inspiring books because that's what drives me and gives me ideas. They inspire me to head in the right direction.*

*I'm in shape and feel good about myself. I go for a daily walk and cleanse my mind, letting any trapped energy out. It feels good to let anxiety and stress out just by moving my feet.*

*I practice good manners and respect everyone I meet.*

*I program my mind with positive programming.*

*I learn from my successful failures. I look fear straight in the eye and declare,*

*"I don't need you. I'm putting faith in front of me. I'm going to achieve anything I want to do because you're nothing however false evidence appearing real. You don't exist." And faith is a fierce attitude in the heart.*

*I ask for help whenever I need it. I face myself in the mirror and say,*

*"I can achieve anything."*

*I use my common sense. I let my intuition tell me what's right and what's wrong. I live my dreams and live them the way I want. I live every day as if it were my last day.*

*I live my possibilities.*

# KEEP YOUR MOMENTUM GOING

To maintain your motivational journey it is absolutely essential that you commit yourself to constant learning. I became convinced of this after hearing a simple story many years ago. I want to share it with you.

There are two goddesses that all of us chase: The Goddess of Wisdom & Knowledge, and the Goddess of Money. Many people think the easiest way to success is to chase the Goddess of Money however she delights in teasing you.

If you chase the Goddess of Wisdom & Knowledge, the Goddess of Money starts to get jealous. The more you pay attention to the Goddess of Wisdom & Knowledge, the more money the Goddess of Money starts throwing your way. She'll do anything to grab your attention.

She'll start throwing so much money at you that you won't know how to react. She'll start giving fistfuls of money to you without playing any games. However, if you give her any attention, she'll run away and start playing games with you again.

What's the moral of this story?

Keep your focus on the Goddess of Wisdom & Knowledge so the Goddess of Money will always throw that money at you. Don't focus solely on money because wisdom and knowledge is what makes the difference. Remember, money is just applause for a job well done.

# GIULIO'S FAVORITE RESOURCES

To get you started increasing your wisdom, I have created a list of resources. These represent some of my favorite books, audio and video collections, movies, and websites. I encourage you to be open to other resources that will motivate and inspire you. Search for other items that move you – however most importantly – don't forget to act! Dive in! Read and experience! What works for you may not work for others, so take the initiative to keep researching.

## BOOKS

Beck, Martha. *Finding Your Own North Star: Claiming the Life You Were Meant to Live*. New York: Three Rivers Press, 2002.

Carnegie, Dale. *How to Win Friends and Influence People.* New York: Simon and Schuster, 1937.

Claybaugh, Winn. *Be Nice or Else*. Laguna Beach: Von Curtis Publishing, 2004.

Collins, Jim. *Good to Great: Why Some Companies Make the Leap... and Others Don't.* New York: Harper Business, 2001.

Covey, Stephen R. *The 7 Habits of Highly Effective People.* Glencoe: Free Press, 1990. (Revised edition 2004).

Gitomer, Jeffrey. *Little Red Book of Selling: 12.5 Principles of Sales Greatness.* Austin: Bard Press, 2004.

Gladwell, Malcolm. *The Tipping Point: How Little Things Can Make a Big Difference.* Boston: Back Bay Books, 2002.

Johnson, Spencer. *Who Moved My Cheese? An Amazing Way to Deal with Change in Your Work and in Your Life.* New York: G. P.

Putnam's Sons, 1998.

Kouzes, James M. and Posner, Barry Z. *The Leadership Challenge*. New York: Jossey-Bass, 1987 (4th edition 2008).

Navarro, Peter. *Always a Winner: Finding Your Competitive Advantage in an Up and Down Economy*. New York: Wiley, 2009.

Patterson, Kerry. *Crucial Conversations*. New York: McGraw-Hill, 2002.

Tracy, Brian. *Eat That Frog! 21 Great Ways to Stop Procrastinating and Get More Done in Less Time.* San Francisco: Berrett-Koehler Publishers, 2007.

Ziglar, Zig. *See You at the Top, (25th Anniversary Edition).* New Orleans: Pelican Publishing, 2000.

## DVDs and CDs:

Canfield, Jack. *The Success Principles. How to Get From Where You Are to Where You Want to Be*. New York: Harper Audio, 2004.

Dyer, Dr. Wayne W. *Excuses Begone! How to Change Lifelong, Self-Defeating Thinking Habits* (Eight CD set). Carlsbad, CA: Hay House, 2009.

Hill, Napoleon. *Think and Grow Rich* (10 CD set). London: Briggs International, 2006.

Hopkins, Tom. *Audio Sales Collection*. New York: Harper Audio, 2002.

Peale, Dr. Norman Vincent. *The Power of Positive Thinking*. New York: Simon & Schuster Audio, 1999.

Peale, Dr. Norman Vincent. *You Can If You Think You Can*. New York: Simon & Schuster Audio, 2005.

Robbins, Anthony. *Unlimited Power!* New York: Simon & Schuster, 2000.

Waitley, Denis. *The Psychology of Winning*. Niles: Nightingale-Conant, 2005.

Ziglar, Zig. *How to Get What You Want.* New York: Simon & Schuster Audio, 2004.

Ziglar, Zig, *Success and the Self-Image*. Niles: Nightingale-Conant, 2002.

Canfield, Jack. *The Success Principles.* Minneapolis: Better Life Media, 2006.

Rohn, Jim. *Living an Exceptional Life.* Minneapolis: Better Life Media, 2004.

Robbins, Anthony. *Personal Power, Classic Edition.* Los Angeles: Guthy Renker, 1996.

Tracy, Brian. *Secrets of Self-Made Millionaires*. Minneapolis: Better Life Media, 2005.

## MOVIES

*The Secret.* TS Production LLC., 2006.

*A Beautiful Mind.* Universal Studios, 2001.

*Billy Elliot.* Universal Studios, 2000.

*Coach Carter.* Paramount, 2005.

*Erin Brockovich.* Universal Studios, 2000.

*Freedom Writers.* Paramount, 2007.

*Pay It Forward.* Warner Brothers, 2001.

*Pursuit of Happyness.* Sony Pictures, 2007.

*Radio.* Sony Pictures, 2004.

*Rudy.* Sony Pictures, 1993

*The Bucket List.* Warner Home Video, 2008.

*The Hurricane.* Universal Studios, 2000.

## WEBSITES

When you start being nice, everyone wins - http://www.beniceorelse.com

Tools for your mind, soul and spirit - http://www.cedarfire.com

Relaxation music, positive affirmations and online counseling - http://www.enhancedhealing.com

Maximizing your Potential - http://www.jackcanfield.com

The Ultimate Resource for Personal Development - http://www.jimrohn.com

Life is Sweet! Certified Business and Life Strategies - http://www.liferecreated.com

The Gift of Inspiration - http://www.simpletruths.com

Life on Your Terms - http://www.tonyrobbins.com

Revolutionary Corporate Training, Sales Motivation, Sales Training Seminars, Management Training Programs & More - http://www.ziglar.com

# Unwrapping Your Gift

# SUMMARY OF THE THIRTY STEPS

## Your Quick Guide

Step 1: Stop Procrastinating

Step 2: Finish What You Start

Step 3: Take Action

Step 4: Ask for Help

Step 5: Dress Up and Stand Tall

Step 6: Your Value Never Depreciates

Step 7: Laugh Often

Step 8: Be a Quitter (and a Loser)

Step 9: Get in Shape

Step 10: Wear a Big Smile

Step 11: Cleanse Your Mind

Step 12: Listen and Read

Step 13: Use Common Sense as Your Compass

Step 14: Find a Mentor

Step 15: Make Your Failures Successful

Step 16: Face Your FEAR

Step 17: NO More Negativity

Step 18: Focus on your Qualities

Step 19: Look Yourself in the Eyes

Step 20: Carry on a Conversation with Yourself

Step 21: Mind Your Manners

Step 22: Control Your Emotions

Step 23: Love Everyone

Step 24: Give More of Yourself

Step 25: Honor Every Relationship

Step 26: Hang with the Best

Step 27: Make Deliberate Choices

Step 28: Stay Focused

Step 29: Visualize Your Dream

Step 30: Live Your Dreams

# Unwrapping Your Gift

# ACKNOWLEDGMENTS

This book has been the result of interactions with many incredible people who have influenced me over my lifetime. Even the briefest of meetings have sometimes ended with positive results that caused me to learn something, be inspired or gain information.

While there are far too many to mention here, I want to emphasize how much I appreciate and value each and everyone's contribution to my life. In some cases, your words or actions even changed my life. I hope they will now change the lives of many more.

I will always acknowledge my mother and father in everything I have ever done. Their sacrifice, love and unending support represent a continual force for good.

My sons have inspired me more than I could have ever hoped, or imagined. Most importantly, I honor my wife for her unconditional love.

I am grateful for the understanding that everyone we encounter has something to teach us. I am committed to be an exemplary teacher to all those who cross my path.

Unwrapping Your Gift

# Illustrator Bio
# Glenn Brown

age: 24
from Schenectady, NY
graduated from UCF with a B.S. in Sports & Exercise Science

Since I was a kid, I've had a passion for drawing and art. It's always come so natural to me and it was a talent that I did not want to waste. Aside from just drawing for fun, I've expanded my skill for the business world. This is my first illustrated book and I'm so incredibly proud of it.

My artwork ranges from anything; cartoons, caricatures, pencil sketches, portraits, logos, designs, and digital art. There's no limit to what I can draw or create. It's my passion to create. I hope to share my talents and collaborate with other creative professionals in all walks of businesses (large & small).

I am very versatile and with my vivid imagination, I can bring any creative vision to life, including YOURS! I've drawn custom artwork for several businesses, including one which is a multi-billion $ company. I've also created a ton of drawings, portraits, caricatures, logos, and tattoo designs for family and friends which is such a pleasure for me.

Throughout my entire life I've created so many drawings and different pieces of art that have had my heart and soul poured into them. My passion drives me to draw more and more. I will never stop. It's fun and it's my career.

I hope to illustrate more and more books in the years to come, as well as to create artwork in many other aspects of business, retail, display, and other services.

GLENN BROWN
"NOOCH"
DIRECTOR/ARTIST
CREATOR/OWNER

GBFILM&ART
gbfna@aol.com
facebook.com/gbfna

# Unwrapping Your Gift

## BRING GIULIO VEGLIO TO YOUR ORGANIZATION OR COMPANY

Through his company, Visionary Freak, Giulio Veglio travels the world sharing his insights to motivate and inspire others. He is fun, high energy and very engaging. It's no wonder that Giulio is highly sought after to appear at conferences, events and special programs as a keynote speaker and workshop presenter. Find out more about his presentations and availability by calling **866-998-4226** or e-mail *info@visionaryfreak.com*.

### START LISTENING TO GIULIO'S TWO POWERFUL CDS TODAY!

*1. Unwrapping Your Gift: Make the Most of Yourself!*

Follow along with Giulio in this two-CD set as he covers the 25 steps to success. Practical tips and suggestions that truly work for everyone.

BRING GIULIO VEGLIOTO YOUR ORGANIZATION OR COMPANY

*2. Rhythm of Success: The Power of Verbal
and Non-Verbal Communication*
Giulio describes effective techniques
to empower hairdressers to become more
successful by developing outstanding in-
terpersonal skills. A perfect guide to catch
your rhythm of success when serving customers.

Both CDs and this book are available in bulk quantity discounts
for reselling, gifts or fundraising. For more information, call **866-
998-4226** or e-mail **info@visionaryfreak.com**.

To keep up with Giulio's programs and activities, visit
**www.visionaryfreak.com**.